Sisters in Law

GW00703326

Also by Elizabeth Cruickshank

Women in the Law
published by Law Society Publishing

Sisters in Law
Career Choices for Nigerian Women Lawyers

BOMA OZOBIA &
ELIZABETH CRUICKSHANK

ISBN 0-9554336-0-6
© Boma Ozobia & Elizabeth Cruickshank

Published in 2006 by
PZ Publishing, 22 Station Road, Dunton Green,
Sevenoaks, Kent TN13 2XA
Printed by Biddles Ltd. Kings Lynn, Norfolk

Dedication

To our husbands, Ikemefuna and Don,
who shared our ambitions for this book

Contents

Foreword

I am delighted to have been asked to write the foreword to this fascinating book. The women that you will read about provide an inspiration to us all in how we should think about and contribute to society. They show that lawyers have much more to offer than advice on the law.

The Nigerian legal profession has impressed me over the years with the strength of its voice, its independence and its professionalism. It has had no hesitation in standing up for the rule of law, for the ending of corruption and for human rights. I first encountered women lawyers in Nigeria when they played a key and highly specialised role in opening up the energy sector – a sector that is typically considered to be quite unsuitable for women! Women lawyers have enabled Nigeria to sustain economic development and to attract much needed investment. In short, as you will see from this book, they have not only made a huge contribution to the justice system and to the welfare of Nigerian women and children, they have done much more. We have a great deal to learn from them.

This book has been written by two past Chairwomen of the Association of Women Solicitors and this foreword by another past Chairwoman, who all passionately believe in the equality and diversity agenda. The fact that I am only the second woman President of the Law Society indicates that we still have a long way to go. To make the most of what women lawyers have to offer we need a complete culture change. In order to encourage them to contribute the most that they can to the profession and to the community we need to examine carefully the way that we think about staff retention and career advancement.

Reading about the way the women in this book have lived their lives and made a mark on society invites us to think differently about just these issues. It's not enough to think simply about flexible working practices and returner courses, valuable as they are. The real agenda involves a culture change where women are empowered to do a meaningful and satisfying job and without the application of a stigma to those who opt for alternative ways of working.

This book reads like a good novel. I am happy to be associated with it and to commend it to you.

Fiona Woolf
President of the Law Society of England and Wales

Acknowledgements

Many people have helped us to make this book possible, and to them we extend our gratitude, because truly without them this book would have languished only in our imaginations.

In Nigeria George Etomi not only lent us his extensive telephone directory to enable contact with many of those interviewed for this book but actively interceded on more than one occasion to persuade these very busy women to spare the time for the interviews. J.B. Daudu SAN patiently assisted us with information on SAN selection criteria. Patience Saduwa undertook the initial research and procured one of the interviews, and young Alice transcribed the interviews from tape to initial draft. Salomey Anthony-Ukpo not only facilitated one of the interviews but also took the time to accompany Boma several hundreds of miles by air and road to make sure that she got there safely and in good order. Sino Kehinde our photographer took the wonderful pictures for this book. Moses navigated the Lagos traffic safely and with minimum fuss to ensure that appointments were kept on time every time. We also thank Barrister M.K. Jibril and M.J. Zubair for their help with arranging one of the interviews.

In the United Kingdom Stephen and Stuart Edwards, our publishers and Nik Harber, our Art Editor, counselled and advised us through the whole publishing process and agreed to do without week-ends to make sure that our book was well designed and most importantly produced on time.

You have helped to make the writing and production of this book a joy and for this we thank you.

Boma Ozobia   **Elizabeth Cruickshank**

About the Authors

Boma
Ozobia

B oma Ozobia was admitted to the Nigerian Bar in 1988 and more recently as a solicitor in England and Wales. She holds a Masters in Maritime Law from King's College, University of London, and is an accredited Civil and Commercial Mediator.

She is a founding partner of Sterling Partnership Solicitors LLP, an international law firm and was Chairwoman of the Association of Women Solicitors of England and Wales in 2005. She received the Art For Behavioural Change Foundation Award as an agent for positive change in Nigerian Society in 2006, and was also given the Nigerian Community Newspaper Award in London for "outstanding professional services."

She is married to Chief Ikemefuna Ozobia and has one son.

Elizabeth Cruickshank

Elizabeth Cruickshank graduated from the University of Aberdeen with two degrees in English Language and Literature. After teaching English for ten years, she re-qualified as a solicitor and worked for three major law firms in the City of London before embarking on a third career as a writer.

She is the Editor of Link, the magazine of the Association of Women Solicitors of England and Wales, and the author of "Women in the Law." She was Chairwoman of the Association of Women Solicitors in 2004, and in 2005 was given the Eva Crawley Award for services to women solicitors.

She is married to Sir Don Cruickshank and has two children and three grandchildren.

Introduction

*Although born in different continents Boma, my co-author,
and I have several things in common.*

Both of us qualified as lawyers in the United Kingdom, although Boma also qualified in Nigeria. Both of us have served as Chairwomen of the Association of Women Solicitors in England and Wales, an honour of which we are both very proud. And we both believe passionately in the right of women to have a sound education and to use their skills for the benefit of their communities, whether in the Northern or the Southern hemispheres.

Genesis and purpose

In 2003 I published a book entitled "Women in the Law" about the achievements of several highly qualified and prominent UK women lawyers. The interviews which were at the core of the book covered women in private practice, women in-house counsel, women who were Government Ministers, women in the judiciary, including Lady Hale, at that time a judge in our Court of Appeal and now the first woman judge to be appointed to our House of Lords, the equivalent of the Supreme Court in Nigeria. To me they were an inspiration and I was very privileged to be able to listen to their descriptions of their careers and their thoughts about women's position in the legal profession.

When Boma suggested that we might collaborate on a book whose purpose would be to extol the careers of women lawyers in Nigeria, I felt that this was a fine opportunity to learn more about women lawyers in another country and indeed in another continent, and to find out if there were differences between our motivations and our achievements, between our successes and our difficulties. It has been a great privilege to participate in this project with Boma, and I am sincerely grateful to all those busy and successful women who gave up their time to be interviewed.

This book is therefore a celebration of those women lawyers in Nigeria, whether in private practice or in commerce or as members of the judiciary, who have made a real difference to the position of women and to the regard in which the Law is held. We have learned so much from being able to speak to them about their careers and in some cases the real struggles that they have had to attain their present positions.

It is also intended as an encouragement to young women who have either already embarked on a career in the Law or who are considering doing so. The message that you will take away from this book is that the Law is a challenging profession. But you should not give up. Look for the niche that will suit you best, whether it be as an attorney in a large firm or as a magistrate in a rural location, and rejoice in the diversity of your opportunities.

Similarities

What certainly unites the women in this book and the women in my earlier book is a concern about the future of justice and the rule of law. In both our countries the Law is regarded as the safeguard of the rights of the individual, and in both the best lawyers are concerned that our profession should not be perverted to take away these rights or used for individual aggrandisement. It is to the great credit of the women in this book that so many of them were prepared to stand up for the rights of others, and particularly for the rights of the oppressed and disadvantaged.

The other great similarity is the willingness of women lawyers everywhere to work hard at their chosen profession while keeping a sense of perspective and being willing to put children and family first. It is of note that nearly all the women interviewed for this book had something to say about the relative balance to be struck between work and family. The Nigerian extended family structure may help with the raising of children, but those children were very much placed centre stage by their hard-working and successful mothers.

This is one message that came across very loud and clear, that having a brilliant mind is not sufficient, and in fact may not be necessary. What is required is integrity, commitment and a willingness to work hard, very hard indeed.

Differences

The motivations of proud women lawyers the world over are in many ways very similar, and some of the experiences of Nigerian women lawyers echo those of their English counterparts. All emphasised the fascination of Law, its ability to help society and none underestimated the hard work required to succeed in it. Family support has been essential, although in some cases and in both countries the choice of career has been very much dictated by parental wishes, usually those of the father.

One of the major differences however, is that there is probably a stronger sense of "giving back to the community" stated as a major reason for entering the profession. This I would ascribe to two causes.

At the time that most of the women lawyers interviewed for this book were entering the Law (mainly in the Nineteen Seventies) there was an explosion in the number of women entering the legal profession in the United Kingdom, whereas in Nigeria there appears have been still very few women lawyers. Consequently women lawyers in Nigeria have had to face sometimes outright prejudice against women in their profession and sometimes prejudice disguised as concern. Overcoming the bias of tradition and culture requires strength and determination, more likely perhaps to come from a strong sense of altruism.

This altruism probably also derived from what I perceive to be the sense of responsibility towards others within their communities and local area generated by centuries of a social framework which equates privilege with responsibility. Thus qualifying as a lawyer and entering a "certain echelon of society" as one interviewee put it, also entailed an obligation to help the wider community. We in the United Kingdom have gone a long way down the road of relying on the state rather than those in our own communities for help. Now that we have so many women lawyers in the United Kingdom the legal profession can be seen as much more of a "job," as a way of earning a living for yourself and your family within the community.

The second is that Nigeria has unfortunately had a much more turbulent political life than the United Kingdom during the time when women were beginning to make inroads into the legal profession. The need for concerned lawyers willing to help others less fortunate than themselves is more immediate and obvious, and the women in this book have certainly risen to that challenge. I hope that they will forgive us that we have not had the space to list all their charitable and pro bono work.

There are differences between English lawyers and Nigerian lawyers in terms of training and therefore also work experience. The legal profession in Nigeria is unified in that all lawyers qualify as having rights of audience in the courts. In the United Kingdom lawyers have until fairly recently been strictly separated into two branches. A rough distinction would be to say that barristers on the whole represent their clients in court whereas solicitors are more concerned with drawing up documents and negotiating on their behalf. Similarly, it is at present almost impossible for a solicitor or indeed a magistrate to attain the position of judge in the High Court, whereas this would be a recognised career possibility in Nigeria.

Much to admire

What I most admire is the determination of Nigerian women lawyers to carry on in a time of political upheaval, in many cases in the face not only of prejudice but of physical threat. Women lawyers in the UK would be surprised at the hints that are dropped here and there in this book about these difficulties, the need to build up your own legal library, the need for standby generators and in some cases the need to conceal yourself from the forces of military dictatorship. It is impossible not to admire their courage in completing their education in the face of extraordinary difficulties, and continuing to practise and to represent others even when they themselves were threatened with imprisonment and worse.

I also admire the support that they have received from the men in their families. Supporting their daughters' ambitions, and in many cases encouraging them to have them in the first place was not exactly what I had anticipated in such a traditional society, which is why it is so important that we speak to each other across international boundaries. It has also become clear that these women were fortunate to have the support of some very enlightened husbands who were, against all my expectations and against established cultural norms, willing to take their share of child care.

And the sheer energy of these women! As well as bringing up children, setting up their own practices, writing their judgments in long hand and travelling large distances in order to represent their clients, they have found time to join and be very active in all sorts of political and charitable ventures. The brief indications of why they were chosen for interview at the head of each interview cannot do justice to all the organisations in which they are involved.

This book is truly the result of cross-continental collaboration, being written partly in Nigeria and partly in the United Kingdom. And what I personally have learned as the result of this experience, and what I hope that our readers will take away from this book, is that Nigerian women lawyers are a force to be reckoned with.

Elizabeth Cruickshank

Iagree with all that my co-author has said and will only add that for me, this has been the culmination of a dream. From the very first time I read his words I have been inspired by John F. Kennedy's injunction that we ask not what our country can do for us, but rather what we can do for our country This has struck a particular chord whenever I reflect on the number of lives lost in our recent history in a bid to "Go on with one Nigeria."

The women lawyers in this book and others whom I have met in the process of researching this project give me hope that this young nation will grow into a strong and responsible adult in the Commonwealth and in the wider world.

I hope young students and others reading this book will be inspired to emulate these sterling examples and indeed aspire to exceed them. I am certainly inspired and can honestly say that in setting out to give this gift to Nigeria I have received far more in return.

Boma Ozobia

Starting a profession –
the first British women lawyers

Background

It is important to note that the legal profession in the United Kingdom has two branches. Lawyers can be either barristers or solicitors. There are many differences between these two branches relating to training and the functions they perform, but in many ways the most obvious division between them is not to do with the amount of time that they spend in court, but with their financial arrangements.

Barristers work independently and do not usually enter into formal written contracts with their clients, most usually obtained through solicitors, for the provision of their services. Solicitors, on the other hand, are regarded as "public-facing" and are bound by legislation to enter into detailed contractual arrangements with their clients before giving advice and performing services for them. Barristers are almost always self-employed, which means that they usually share offices and staff on a cost-sharing rather than a fee-sharing basis, which can make it particularly hard for young barristers starting out on their careers. Solicitors on the other hand usually start out as the employees of other solicitors or organisations who bear the brunt of office costs. Until solicitors become partners in a legal partnership they will have no responsibility for office expenses but will be entitled only to their fixed salary, perhaps an annual bonus, but no share in the profits generated by the partnership.

In the public eye barristers are associated with advocacy and court work and solicitors with office work. This is true as a rough and ready distinction, but it is one that has been steadily eroded in the solicitors' favour over the past decade or so. Solicitors have always had rights of audience in the lower, magistrates, courts, but now an increasing number are obtaining "higher rights of audience" which enables them to represent their clients in the High Court. They have also increasingly been seen as a source of recruits to the magistracy and the judiciary at the lower level, although the higher ranks of the judiciary in the Court of Appeal and the House of Lords are still very much the preserve of the barristers' profession.

At present there are over 100,000 solicitors holding certificates entitling them to practise in England and Wales (Practising Certificates) of whom 41.6% are women. There are almost 15,000 practising barristers, of whom 32.9% are women.

Rejection in principle

In December 1911 a leading lady lawyer gave a lecture at Marble Arch House, London, where she advocated the right of women to sit on juries. She believed that "they had qualities which would be extremely serviceable if employed in this way. They had great powers of intuition and it was essentially this which was needed by jurors." She also stated that women should employ gentleness rather than violence in arguing for their rights. "It is clumsy to treat men as the irreconcilable enemies of women. Feminism, rightly understood, is less a blind hatred of the rights of men than the safeguarding of those of women by wise enactments. Along these lines women would always triumph."

The same publication which had reported the words of this lecture also reported on 16 March 1912 that "a lady having applied to enter for the preliminary examination of the Law Society, the Council resolved, on the recommendation of the Examination Committee that following a previous report of the Committee dated the 1st of June 1904, on the same subject, the applicant be informed that the Council do not see their way to allow a woman to enter for examination or to register articles of clerkship with a view to admission as a solicitor."

The apparent inconsistency between these two statements is easily resolved, when one realises that the lawyer secure in her profession advocating the rights of women to become jurors, was in fact a French lady *avocate*. The French were certainly ahead of the British in appreciating the legal skills of women, although the British were not so backward in acknowledging the competence of women in other professional spheres.

Women had been practising as doctors in the UK since the middle of the Nineteenth Century, but it was not until half a century later that they were permitted to practise as lawyers. And even then the UK was not setting an example to the rest of the English-speaking world, as by then the United States in 1869, Canada in 1879 and New Zealand in 1896 had all registered their first female lawyers.

The Bebb Case

Since 1879 women had been attempting to enter the legal profession in the UK, when a young lady was refused permission by the Law Society to sit its examinations. Between 1875 and the early 1880s Miss Eliza Orme and Miss M E Richardson opened a legal office in Chancery Lane. Although neither of them could officially practise, they were in effect legal assistants to solicitors and members of the Bar. Many years later one male solicitor admitted that Eliza Orme was "unquestionably a very able lawyer and expert conveyancer, and would, I think, had she been able to be called to the Bar as was her wish, have greatly distinguished herself in the profession."

By the early 1900s thinking women wanted not only to be able to vote in the UK but to have access to the machinery and process of the law. In 1900 a Scotswoman, Margaret Hall, applied to the Society of Law Agents in Scotland for permission to take their entrance examination. Her application was rejected by the Society and subsequently by the Scottish Courts on the grounds that the term "persons" in the legislation governing entry to the profession applied only to "male persons."

Things began to move forward when in 1913 four highly educated young women applied to the Law Society of England and Wales for permission to study for and to sit the Law Society exams. They were Gwynneth Bebb, Karin Costelloe who later became Mrs Adrian Stephens, and thus one of the Bloomsbury Group, Maud Ingram (later Crofts), and Lucy Nettlefold. Despite having First Class degrees they were refused on the grounds that according to common law a woman was "incapable of carrying out a public function." Undeterred they took the Law Society to Court.

They lost in the High Court. Then they appealed to the Court of Appeal. Their Lordships were required to interpret the provisions of the Solicitors Act 1729 as subsequently amended. The young women asked the Court to construe the relevant section in accordance with the provisions of the Interpretation Act 1891. Section 1 of that act stated that the masculine provision in statutes should be construed to contain the feminine. By the time this case was heard, the Interpretation Act had been in operation for a good 20 years, so that the conclusion that women could be solicitors might have seemed inevitable.

In coming to its decision in *Bebb v Law Society [1914] 1 Ch 286* the Court of Appeal accepted the arguments of the Law Society, one of whose counsel relied indirectly on the authority of a mediaeval treatise entitled "The Mirror of Justices" which stated that "all who are not prohibited by law may be attorneys but the law will not suffer women to be attorneys nor infants nor serfs." Ultimately the Court of Appeal was not prepared to upset a practice of very long standing on the strength of the "relatively recent" Interpretation Act. They concluded that women did not fall within the definition of "persons" for the purposes of the Solicitors Acts, and therefore that women, like serfs and children, lacked the legal capacity to become solicitors or barristers.

The Bar was no more enlightened. In 1903 Bertha Cave had applied to Gray's Inn for admission as a student. Although initially the Benchers of Gray's Inn were minded to admit her, they felt that they should apply to the Courts for clarification. And the Courts decided against her admission.

The Influence of the 1914-1918 War

Women might have pursued their rights to equality in the law more vigorously had not the 1914-18 war intervened, for in 1913 a *Legal Profession (Admission of Women) Bill* had been put forward for Parliamentary consideration. This was opposed by the Law Society and the Bar, but with the coming of peace it was appreciated that not only had women enabled the legal work of the country to continue by staffing legal offices, but that they would be necessary for the continuation of the legal profession after the death of so many young men in the trenches.

During the War the attitude of the legal profession and the legal press had changed substantially, and The Law Times of 1 February 1919 declared that "during the war we were strongly opposed to the admission of women to the Profession, and this view was generally held. But with the coming of peace the whole subject must be considered in view of the facts of the last four years and provided the interests of those students and younger members of both branches who have served their country are duly looked after, the time is arriving when the doors of the profession should be opened to all persons irrespective of sex."

The Sex Disqualification (Removal) Act 1919

On 28 March 1919 the Law Society called a Special General Meeting where it was resolved by a majority of 59 to 38 "that in view of the present economic and political position of women, it is in the opinion of this meeting expedient that the existing obstacles to their entry to the legal profession should be removed." *The Sex (Disqualification) Removal Act 1919* which permitted women to hold any office or to enter or carry on any civil profession or vocation became law on 23 December 1919 and was welcomed by the Law Society and the Bar.

Further ramifications of the Act

The ramifications of this Act were not confined to the legal profession. Maud Crofts noted in her 1928 book "Women Under English Law" that women were now able to become members of the professional associations of accountants, actuaries, architects, surveyors, veterinary surgeons and almost all engineering associations and societies. Like female doctors and teachers they were now eligible to train for and to enter the ranks of the professions. There were still, however, some areas where women's progress was restricted. The passage of the Act might have opened the way to women to enter all the professions, but power was reserved to appoint men only to posts in the Colonial and Indian Civil Service and to the diplomatic corps.

The 1919 Act also enabled women to serve on juries. Previously the only jury on which women could serve was a "Jury of Matrons." This was convened where a woman who was in custody and legally condemned to die claimed that she was pregnant. If the Jury of Matrons ascertained that she was indeed pregnant her execution could be postponed until after the birth of the child. In practice in such a case her sentence was usually commuted to penal servitude for life. But of course only a jury of men could have found her guilty in the first place of the crime of which she was accused. The Act thus enabled women to become jurors and in principle at least they had the same power over men's futures that men had over women's.

Very soon after the passing of the Act the Lord Chancellor appointed 200 women magistrates, but it took 14 years before the number of women solicitors reached that number. Educated women were presumably willing to take on this responsibility because, although magistrates were unpaid, it was not a prerequisite that they had undergone expensive training such as the barristers and solicitors who appeared before them were required to do.

The first women lawyers

Twelve women registered as articled clerks with the Law Society in 1919 and in its 1923 Annual Report the Law Society was pleased to report that four women had now been admitted to the profession.

These women were Carrie Morrison, Maud Crofts, Mary Sykes and Mary Pickup, and three of them (Maud Crofts, Mary Sykes and Mary Pickup) had obtained Honours in the Law Society Finals examination. At the same time Ivy

Williams had the honour of being the first woman to be called to the Bar, but as she immediately returned to an academic life in Oxford, it was Helena Normanton who became in 1922 the first woman to practise as a barrister. Normanton was a remarkable woman who in 1924 fought to become the first married woman to be able to travel on her own passport under her maiden name. In 1949 she and Rose Heilbron became the first women King's Counsel (the equivalent of an SAN in Nigeria), and Heilbron later went on to become the first woman judge to sit at the Old Bailey.

Carrie Morrison was the first woman actually to be admitted as a solicitor in December 1922. A graduate of Girton College, Cambridge, she had served during the 1914-18 War in the War Office and the Army of the Black Sea at Constantinople. She practised until she died aged 62 on 20 February 1950 at 7 New Square. A woman of stout views her primary concern was with Family Law and in 1933 she spoke on the topic of the reform of the law appertaining to married women. She thought that women ought to take the rough with the smooth and to bear their due share of the joint burdens. She also advocated that housekeeping money given to a wife by her husband should be the wife's own property, and argued against the law which required a husband to be liable for his wife's tax even though she made a separate tax return. Perhaps ahead of their time she and her husband Ambrose Applebe argued in 1939 for a solicitors' fund to be set up to indemnify individuals against loss connected with solicitors' defalcations.

Maud Crofts was the only one of the four women involved with the Bebb case who subsequently qualified as a solicitor. The daughter of a barrister, she could have lived a comfortable life of ease after gaining Honours in the History and Law Tripos at Girton College, Cambridge. Instead, a life-long advocate of women's suffrage, she was the first woman to take out a Practising Certificate and set up in practice with her brother and her husband under the name of Crofts, Ingram and Wyatt & Co. Wealthy and influential members of the women's suffrage movement in which she had been prominent formed an instant and loyal clientele. In order to accommodate her family responsibilities (she met her children from school at 4 pm every day) the partnership was structured so that she had a one-fifths share against two-fifths each of her husband and her brother. She continued to practise until 1955, when in a neat instance of reverse discrimination, several of her clients, not wishing to be advised by a man, took their business elsewhere.

Maud Crofts was followed into the profession by her daughter, Rosemary and by her grand-daughter, Mary, the first, and as far as is known, the only family in the UK to produce three generations of female solicitors.

Immediate effects of the 1919 Act

Although women now had the right to enter the legal profession they did not enter it in the droves that some men had feared. The requirement that an articled clerk should pay a training premium made it difficult for women, even middle-class ones, to become solicitors unless they had family connections in the Law. In 1924 anything from £300 to £500 might be required as a premium, at a time when the salary for a newly qualified solicitor was £150-£250 per year. This financial burden was further exacerbated by the £80 Stamp Duty on articles, the £25 Duty on admission and the £9 Duty on Practising Certificates required by the Government. These duties were not abolished until 1949 and indeed some solicitors alive to-day can remember paying the Stamp Duty on Articles even when they were not asked for a training premium.

On the other hand partners in small law firms saw training their daughters themselves as a way of ensuring that their daughters were financially independent when they could not afford to send them to University.

Within this context it is perhaps not surprising that only 136 women qualified as solicitors in the ten years between 1922 and 1932. What is perhaps more surprising is that by 1952 only 382 women had qualified. In fact during that time the only years when the number of women passing the Finals as a percentage of the total number passing reached double figures was during the 1939-1945 War. The explosion in the number of women holding Practising Certificates began in the Nineteen Seventies and has rapidly gained momentum since 1987. As recently as 1967, only 619 women or 2.7% of the total profession held Practising Certificates.

In the early years women joined the Bar in roughly the same numbers as they became solicitors. In the 20 years post 1922 on average 13 women a year qualified as solicitors and 13 women a year qualified as barristers. Because the Bar in total was much smaller this meant that a higher proportion of the total number of barristers was female as opposed to the proportion of solicitors who were women.

Social attitudes and conscience

Not all women practised after qualification. Many "retired" after they married or had children. This should be seen against the background of prevailing social attitudes, which were not totally in favour of professional women in the workplace. Generally practising in small family firms made it easier for women to continue to practise while bringing up their families. The majority of women who went into partnership between 1922 and 1962 went into what were obviously family firms, often joining their husbands or fathers, brothers or uncles. There were however, several instances of all women partnerships. One notable partnership formed in the Thirties was that between Beatrice Davy and Madge Easton Anderson on her re-qualification as an English solicitor. Miss Anderson was a Scotswoman who by qualifying in Scotland in 1920 was in fact the first woman recognised as qualifying as a solicitor in the UK.

Women solicitors were certainly in a more privileged position than some. During the 1939-1944 War when the country suffered from a shortage of educated manpower, female teachers who married were legally required to give up their positions and the Government Legal Service would employ women only if they were "either unmarried or widowed; and will normally be required to resign their appointments on marriage."

Female solicitors on the other hand definitely "kept the home fires burning" during the 1939-1945 War and some like Barbara Littlewood in Guildford not only kept her own family firm going but assisted at the next door firm as well. As 6,124 solicitors and 2,490 articled clerks were at some point engaged in the fighting services during this time, women solicitors and clerks were required everywhere. Some were more actively employed in the War effort, for example as conveyancers within Government departments or indeed involved in work at Bletchley Park, which was a highly secret Government installation devoted to code-breaking.

Why Law?

The movement for women to have the right to train as barristers and solicitors ran almost in parallel with the campaign for women to have the right to vote in Parliamentary elections. Indeed Maud Crofts regarded herself as a "suffragist," who argued and lobbied for women's right to vote as opposed to a "suffragette" who employed more extreme tactics in support of the same end. For educated women of the time the two goals were almost inextricably linked. Women could not have access to justice and rights under the Law if they could not represent themselves and other women both through the legislative process and in the Courts.

But once the enabling legislation had been passed what was it that motivated individual women to become lawyers? The somewhat surprising conclusion is that often the ambition and motivations were not their own, or at least not wholly their own. Very many of the women who qualified during that period had family connections in the profession, and some of the paternal influence that was exerted verged on extreme self-interest.

Career pattern

For a solicitor with his own practice, taking on his daughter as an articled clerk had many advantages. He could provide her with a means of earning a living at small cost to himself at a time when sending her to university would involve fees and living expenses, he could obtain cheap labour in his office and he could keep an eye on her. And when she qualified he had someone who owed him loyalty and who might continue to be paid less than he might have to pay someone else, but would also have a marketable skill which would ensure her financial independence.

Once qualified the new female solicitor's career, or lack of it, was often dictated as much by the exigencies of her husband's career or domestic requirements as by her own ambition. A legal qualification was regarded almost as an insurance policy which could be cashed in when circumstances required. Many of the first women solicitors retired when they married, or certainly when their first child was born, and although many returned to work during the 1939-1945 War to keep their family practices going, they often returned quietly to the home when the War was over.

The Law Society

The Law Society, the governing body of solicitors in England and Wales was initially in difficulties about admitting women to membership as there were inadequate "facilities" but the Council resolved fairly quickly in March 1923 to make "appropriate" accommodation available, including the conversion of a coal store into a retiring room for the exclusive use of women members. Separate accommodation was also made available for women students sitting the Law Society's examinations, as they were not permitted to take them in the same room as male students, presumably in case their feminine charms were a distraction for the susceptible.

It is easy to find much that is at best amusing and at worst patronising in the attitude of the Law Society to its female members in the decades immediately after the passing of the 1919 Act. However, put in the context of the low numbers of women in the profession and the way that society generally viewed women, the position of the Law Society can be seen as bemused and protective. Certainly many young women were lost to the profession through marriage almost before they had begun, but on the other hand male solicitors were faced with some extraordinarily able legal minds who quietly won major Law Society prizes under the noses of the men and in some cases went on to singular success.

As late as the 1950s the Law Society Council contained members who had entered the profession long before the passing of the 1919 Act. Even when they themselves had learned to appreciate the abilities of their female colleagues they were faced with the prejudice of the times, and the ingrained habits of centuries.

In 1955 the President of the Law Society spoke approvingly of the "industry and competence" of lady solicitors, and said that his partner Ivy Gibson, who was also Honorary Secretary of the Associated Law Societies of Wales, had acquired a new client on the advice of her friend who said "you go and see Miss Gibson. She is very clever and nearly as good as a real solicitor." A signal mark of women solicitors' competence was that not until 1941 was a woman solicitor found guilty of professional misconduct and struck off.

For decades after the first woman had qualified, solicitors advertising for young solicitors would blatantly advertise for "public school men," making it quite clear that women would not be considered. And some women solicitors can still remember that they could take their fathers into the Law Society Dining Room as guests but not their mothers. Indeed one solicitor father on being told by the waiting staff that he could not bring a lady guest into the Dining Room said loudly "My daughter is not a lady. She is an articled clerk. "

What of the future?

As the table below will show the number of women solicitors in the UK, so very few at first, have burgeoned over the past thirty years. And this is only part of the story. At present 63.5% of Law students enrolled with the Law Society are women, 62% of trainee solicitors are women and 60% of newly qualified solicitors are women. The less encouraging statistic is that only 23% of partners in law firms are women. There has been considerable debate as to why this figure is so low, and many theories have been put forward ranging from ineradicable male prejudice through the unwillingness of women to commit their family finances to the potential development of their firm's practice to the difficulty of finding good quality childcare and sufficiently flexible workplaces during the years when their children are growing up.

The progress of women in the legal profession has undoubtedly been patchy and unpredictable, but success there has been. In 2002 Carolyn Kirby became the first woman to become President of that very Law Society which had so vigorously rejected women less than a century ago, and in July 2006 Fiona Woolf became the second. We now have women Managing Partners and Senior Partners in some of the largest law firms in the UK, and several women barristers are now among the highest earners at the Bar.

More than 150 women have been appointed as King's Counsel or Queen's Counsel since Helena Normanton and Rose Heilbron first received this accolade in 1949. Now 10.5% of High Court judges are women, 3 out of the 37 Appeal Court Judges are women and at last we have in Brenda Hale the first woman ever to sit in a judicial capacity in the House of Lords.

Much has been achieved, but much is still to be done.

A few facts and figures

	Total Solicitors Holding Practising Certificates	Women Holding Practising Certificates	Women as a Percentage of Solicitors holding Practising Certificates
1957	18,344	356	1.94%
1967	22,233	619	2.70%
1977	32,812	2,408	7.33%
1987	149,937	8,809	18.00%
1997	71,637	23,466	32.75%
2005	100,938	41,967	41.6%

Pioneering Women Lawyers

First men

It is less than a hundred years since records of the formal registration of Nigerian lawyers began. Christopher Alexander Sapara Williams, who was called to the English Bar in 1879, is recognised as the first Nigerian lawyer to practise in Nigeria. As he practised in both Accra and Lagos he must have been particularly well travelled.

First women

The first Nigerian woman lawyer on record was Stella Jane Thomas (nee Marke) who was admitted to practise law on 16 November 1935, but it took more than thirty years before any woman achieved real prominence in the profession. Indeed this did not happen until after Independence, when on 10 November 1969 Modupe Omo-Eboh, who had been called to the Bar on 14 March 1953, became the first female High Court Judge in Nigeria. This incidentally was only 4 years after Elizabeth Lane became the first female High Court Judge in the UK.

Other notable pioneers within the Judiciary include Hon. Justice Roseline Ukeje, who having been called to the Bar on

18 June 1971, became the first woman appointee to the Federal High Court when she was sworn in on 12 November 1986. Currently she is not only the first but also the only female Chief Justice of the Federal High Court in Nigeria, and the President of the National Association of Women Judges, Nigeria.

The first female judge of the Federal Capital Territory, Justice Ayo Uzoamaka Victoria Onejeme, who was called to the Bar on 30 July 1965, was appointed on 12 October 1984. She also holds the distinction of being the first woman to be appointed as an Attorney General in Nigeria, when she held the post of Attorney General, Anambra State.

Up to date

It was not until 2004 that Dame Brenda Hale was elevated to the House of Lords in the United Kingdom, the first female judge ever to attain that distinction. Only a year later, in June 2005, women lawyers in Nigeria reacted with quiet satisfaction to the news of Hon. Justice Aloma Mariam Mukhtar's elevation to the Supreme Court. The founding President of the National Association of Women Judges, Nigeria, Hon. Justice Mukhtar was also the first woman to be appointed to the Court of Appeal in 1987, eighteen long years before her appointment to the Supreme Court.

The general feeling has been that her elevation is a signal that at last Nigerian women lawyers have broken through the final level of their professional glass ceiling. But of course they are now asking the same question that women lawyers are asking in the United Kingdom – Who will be next? As there are now almost 200 female judges out of the present 800 members of the Superior Courts judiciary, perhaps it might not be too long.

Academia

In the academic field, one woman lawyer has consistently blazed a luminous trail for other women lawyers to follow. She is all the more remarkable because in doing so she has consistently made it her purpose to assist and encourage those behind her.

Jadesola Akande is not only a Professor of Law, but was also the first woman lawyer to serve as the Vice-Chancellor of a tertiary institution in Nigeria. Born on 15 November 1940 in Lagos, she attended University College, London, where she obtained both an LL.B (Hons.) and a Ph.D. In 1965, after attending the Nigerian Law School, she was called to the Bar before joining the University of Lagos as an academic staff member.

After becoming a Professor she was elected to the Senate of the University of Lagos from 1979 to 1981, and from 1984 to 1994 was a Research Professor at the Nigerian Institute of Advanced Legal Studies, University of Lagos campus. In addition to her numerous academic achievements, Professor Akande was the Executive Director and founder of the Women, Law and Development Centre (WOLDEC), one of the first Non-Governmental Organisations representing women's interests in Nigeria. She has acted as a consultant to the UNDP, UNICEF and AU on gender issues and was an initiator of a Family Law Centre.

She was a delegate to the 1995 United World Conference on Women in Beijing and has represented women in many other fora since. In recognition of her services to her profession, her country and to women, she was decorated with the Commander of the Order of the Niger (CON) in 1998 and honoured as an Achiever of the International Federation of Women Lawyers in 1989.

SAN status

The first woman lawyer to achieve the status of Senior Advocate of Nigeria is Chief Mrs Folake Solanke SAN who also achieved another notable first as the first woman to be appointed Commissioner in the Western Region of Nigeria as it then was. She is a life patron of FIDA Nigeria and continues to practise in Ibadan, Oyo State. Since Chief Solanke broke through the barrier only five more women have been appointed in the entire history of Nigeria, two of whom are interviewed in this book.

Fati Abubakar

Fati Abubakar is a High Court Judge in Niger State. She was the first woman lawyer to be appointed as the Solicitor-General and subsequently the Attorney-General and Commissioner for Justice of Niger State. She is also the founder of WRAPA (Women's Rights Advancement and Protection Alternative).

As Fati's father was a civil servant she was, from a very young age, alternatively a boarder and a day girl at a Catholic girls school in Kaduna , depending on where her father was posted. The boarding house was very noisy and Fati remembers watching from the gate enviously when day students were picked up in the afternoon. Although it must have been a potentially lonely and isolated time for a little girl brought up in a Muslim household when she was suddenly transplanted to the world of Catholic nuns and boarding schools, Fati insists that "I was not traumatised."

First ambitions

Fati's initial ambition was to read medicine but Physics proved a stumbling block, and she was forced to drop this subject in her Fifth Year at Secondary School. Instead she became enamoured of the words "Sociology and Anthropology," decided that she wanted to study this fine sounding pair of subjects, and when completing the application form for admission into her university of first choice, she grouped them together as her first choice course of study. However when she told her father, he was completely against it and advised her that she would be far better placed for coping with life if she studied a professional course such as Law. Following her father's advice, she then applied to the University of Ife (now Obafemi Awolowo University), this time choosing Law as her first choice subject.

The Law Faculty at Ife University was a friendly place, whose lecturers were quite young and hardworking and very supportive. For three years Fati diligently studied during the week and returned home at the week-end, before graduating in 1975 and subsequently attending the Nigerian Law School. After the intensity of studying at University, Fati did not find Law School very taxing, and she remembers this period in her life as being fairly uneventful, save for a military coup d'etat on what should have been another ordinary day in School. Even such momentous events can be helpful in small ways. The test on Civil Procedure Rules for which she had inadequately prepared was providentially postponed. This gave her a little more time to revise, very useful because as she says, "I was expecting my third child by then."

Marriage and family

After her A Levels and just before she went to University Fati married Abdulsalam Abubakar. As testament to having made the correct choice she now has six children, several grandchildren and her husband publicly supports her work with WRAPA. As testament to her capacity for hard work, by the end of her three years of undergraduate study she had completed her degree and given birth to two children. Her husband, then a young army officer, was stationed in

Benin and therefore a major deciding factor in choosing to study at the University of Ife was its proximity to her marital home. Whatever the reason, the University of Ife in its new incarnation of Obafemi Awolowo University returned the compliment in 2005 by awarding her an Honorary Degree.

The timing of her first daughter's birth was fortuitous as she was born just at the start of the long vacation preceding the new academic year so that by the time Fati had to return to University for her second year of study, her daughter was almost three months old and could be left in the care of her grandmother whilst her young mother returned to school to study. Fati admits that it was very difficult leaving her baby behind although she knew she was well cared for and it is clear that she lived for her weekend trips home to spend time with her family.

In 1976 Fati became the 3847th person to be registered as a lawyer in Nigeria. In keeping with the policy that married women are usually posted to their marital home state or city in order as far as possible to keep families together, Fati was posted by the NYSC to her home town. As her husband had been sent abroad for further military training, Fati opted to be posted to her parental home and immediately started work at the Ministry of Justice. At the time of her graduation the North had become conscious of the hardships suffered by many university students on graduation and offered them employment as administrative clerks within the judicial system.

These in service students, who were also paid a salary, were able to obtain a valuable insight into the workings of the Judiciary. However, when they began their Youth Service year, their salaries and allowances ceased and were replaced by the NYSC allowance. At the Ministry of Justice Fati found herself thrown straight into the deep end after only a couple of appearances in Court with senior lawyers. Although she had spent a few weeks at the Ministry serving her chambers attachment as part of the prequalification requirements of the Law School, that experience had in no way prepared her for the reality of shouldering the full responsibility of presenting a case before a judge. On one particular occasion she remembers that the older lawyer on the other side kept objecting "to every statement I made until eventually the judge intervened with the kindly comment that her opponent should view this as an extension of my Law School training."

Being a woman

Fati says that being female was "never an issue" because she was quietly confident of her abilities and did not feel at a disadvantage in this regard. "Any confidence that I have stems from my upbringing as neither I nor my siblings were made to feel inadequate because of our gender. The difficulties that I encountered in the early days of my career were just what might be expected by any young lawyers honing their advocacy skills and putting in initial appearances in court." Making the quantum leap from theory to practice without much preparation was daunting, but no more daunting than if she had been a young man in the same situation. "You do not want to make mistakes and it is very nerve wracking." Fortunately the judge who dealt with the majority of the cases in her area was a kindly and fatherly man who acted as a mentor and guide to all the young lawyers who appeared before him and who later went on to become the Chief Judge of Niger State when that State was created. The toughest times she faced in court were when she was away from her home patch and this helpful judge, but she soon learned the ropes and began to perform with confidence.

Fati does not recall her mother expressing any opinion about her studies, as "our society is very paternalistic and it was really my father who made decisions affecting the children's lives." But to her mother's credit, she did not try to dissuade young Fati either and left her to get on with her studies in accordance with her father's wishes. On the other hand Fati recalls that her maternal great grandmother called her aside one day when she was a teenager in secondary school Year Three and advised her to "go and tell your father that you don't want to go to school again, because you want to get married." Fati has always been pleased that she had the good sense to reject this unwanted piece of advice. "Studying Law was the best thing I could have done. It's a very satisfying profession, it empowers you and gives you a strong sense of self worth, not in the sense of being arrogant, but in the sense of recognising your value as a human being. Most of all it has given me an opportunity to help others, most especially now that God has chosen to make me a Judge and I make decisions that affect other people's lives."

Gender does play a part in appointments, and perhaps administrative decisions, but Fati believes she has not encountered serious difficulties as a woman lawyer. She says that certainly when you are not known in a jurisdiction and you appear in court for the first time, male colleagues will "test you to see how strong you are." You have to deal with them firmly to establish the mutual respect that forms the basis of any professional interaction.

Being a judge

Fati considers that the high point of her legal career has been her elevation to the High Court as a Judge, which is the culmination of a path leading from a position as a lowly prosecutor within the Ministry of Justice through a stint in private practice and positions as Solicitor General and Attorney General before her judicial appointment. She has also served as a member of the Constituent Assembly and between 1987 and 1989 as a member of the Committee on Constitutional Review, where she helped to contribute to the Nigerian Constitution as it currently stands. "I have learned a lot along the way and met many good people and would not have missed any of these experiences."

Wisdom comes with the ability to assess experience strenuously and to apply it to present and future situations. Fati has used her legal experience well. She describes her life as a judge as a learning process. "Every day you have to learn. Being a judge requires an entirely different skill set from that required for advocacy, and you have to try hard to develop these skills." Sitting as a judge, "I often recollect past scenes in Court when I was a prosecutor and advocate and I can then begin to see it all from another angle. Then I really do understand what happened in the past."

Now that many young advocates appear before her, it is clear that she takes the same attitude as the fatherly judge of many years ago although she does not articulate this. In her capacity as a judge Fati has to hear a wide variety of cases covering every aspect and facet of Law. She says that the greatest resource she has as a judge are the precedents contained in the Law Reports. She says that she also does a lot of research to ensure that she is up to date.

A judge's work

Her judicial working day has a fairly set routine, although the cases that come before her have considerable variety. The day usually starts in her chambers with a review of the files of cases listed for hearing on that day. "Whether it is a good day or a frustrating one depends very much on the advocates appearing before you. There are some who are well prepared and skilled at their craft and these are a pleasure to hear, while others appear ill prepared and ill equipped for the job." She will not brook discourtesy or slovenly dress in her court and will refuse to hear any lawyer who does not meet this minimum professional standard. The most important task for judges is to keep control of their individual courts. "If you do not do that the lawyers will try to dribble past you. They have to know that they must be in court on time, and that if they are not there on time without good reason that you may strike out the case. They have to be prepared and properly turned out. Most importantly, they must abide by the ethics of the profession in their conduct in Court. They have to be polite." She has no time for lawyers who want to play to the gallery and those who think they are so smart that they attempt to overwhelm judges with their supposed knowledge.

A large part of Fati's day is spent writing. "In long hand," she states with great emphasis. Judges write in long hand when Court is in session and later when they prepare their judgements. In some provincial areas where English is not the spoken language of most of the population and everything has to be translated from Hausa, interpreters are required. As Judges must then be especially alert to avoid misinterpretation, they can consequently find themselves becoming interpreters, and effectively "wearing two hats" during Court proceedings. Proceedings that should thus take a short time, take an unduly long time because of the lack of skilled and properly trained interpreters. This places an additional burden on judges in Nigeria which would surprise the judiciary in other jurisdictions

Judicial difficulties

The diminishing resources available to the courts as a result of the recognition and creation of new Nigerian States has had an effect on wages and the competence levels of court employees. This means that "as a judge you may find yourself with an interpreter whose Hausa is fluent but whose command of English is not so fluent, so you have to intervene and assist to ensure that the precise meaning is ascribed to the evidence and that the meaning does not get lost in translation." In some cases the Registrar doubles as the interpreter, but unfortunately may not really have the competence to do so, because interpreting is a very technical job. "Hausa is a very simple language, but it is also a very precise language and a person who is not Hausa may not always understand the precise nuance and therefore the meaning of a word in a particular context as one word lends itself to more than one meaning quite often. That is why I have to spend time to ensure that the witness understands exactly the question that is being put to him to ensure that there is no miscarriage of justice."

Fati has very clear ideas on what would be necessary to improve the working conditions of judges and thus their ability to dispense justice effectively. "The process of judgement has to be made easier on the judge because right now it is very difficult. One of the frustrations of the position is the lack of properly trained support staff. We need to have properly trained and qualified researchers to assist us. Right now what we have are administrative assistants from the Civil Service who may have at the most a Higher Diploma. This means that you cannot rely on them and that you really must do everything yourself. I know that there are plans to ameliorate the situation, but of course there are other priorities for the scarce resources available to the state."

Judicial responsibility

In terms of how well the Judiciary are responding to the needs of civil society and of people generally, Fati comments that "the Courts have to wait for the cases to come to them. By and large the Superior Courts of Record do a very good job because they are very closely monitored and the judgements handed down from these courts are carefully scrutinised. The burden of office and the Judicial Oath is taken very seriously. In the lower ranks, in the magistracy where the bulk of the cases are heard, the challenges are unfortunately somewhat more, because even less support is available to them. As it is, a lot still do what they can but there are a lot of temptations and some magistrates are not able to withstand this. There are a lot of constraints and there is really a need to do more for them so that we properly meet the expectations of the public."

In Fati's opinion "it is the lawyer that really determines how the Court performs. When you have advocates before you who know what they are talking about, it challenges you and it gives you the incentive to do more and in fact eases your work." On the other hand there are some lawyers "who either are not serious or who really do not know the law – and you do have them." In such situations judges have to be very careful not to jump into the arena, even where a lawyer is seriously damaging his client's case. "And sometimes there are certain cases that challenge you morally, but as a judge you can only base your judgement on the evidence. In a society like ours where you have a high rate of illiteracy, lawyers owe a particular duty not to take advantage of such clients, but to be honest in their dealings with them."

Commenting on the Judicial Oath, she says that in practice it is easy to carry out the work without fear or favour "if it does not affect you personally which is why there are rules

governing this aspect and what cases you can hear."
The difficulty arises where you have to resist the temptation
to get involved when you see that, as a result of the actions
of lawyers, justice may not have been done in a particular
case. Judges have the additional pressure of knowing that
they are constantly under observation, and that if they
begin to behave in ways that breach the Oath, it will very
soon come to the attention of the Disciplinary Committee,
resulting in disciplinary measures and potential removal
from the Bench. "As human beings judges will err and a lot
of judgements are over turned as a result of human error but
you should do your job to the best of your ability at all
times. This is where it is up to the individual Judge. You
have to look out for possible conflict of interest in any area
and avoid cases where there might be such a possibility. You
must also be careful how you comport yourself in public,
should maintain a proper distance, and not be over
gregarious as the more you are in contact with people the
more likely they are to try to get to you. So you have to be
careful of your relationships."

What it is to be a lawyer

The legal profession is good for those who are prepared to
be reading constantly and who are ready to abide by the
ethics of the profession. She considers that this is true of the
majority of the profession. "Lawyers are not liars, we have
very high professional standards and in order to be one,
you have to be prepared to be honest, to be hardworking, to
be versatile and to give the profession your best." Fati will
not have any truck with those who consider that the Law is
not a suitable profession for a woman. "Law is a profession
that is certainly not beyond the capabilities of women,
although they do perhaps have to be more determined in

order to combine family life with a career – any career. It is the woman's duty in our society to be the home keeper and this is our most important duty. It may produce some restrictions while building a career. There were times that I was not living with my husband because of his career in the military and surviving the consequent demands – constant travel and movement from place to place - took a very strong relationship. You have to ensure you get your priorities right and do not sacrifice what is most important to you."

Review of the Constitution

Fati was a member of the Committee set up in 1987 to review the 1979 Constitution and to make recommendations about its potential revision but not to draft a new constitution as some people erroneously believed at the time. Forty people were nominated to this important task which was to "renovate" the Constitution and to ensure that all clauses continued to be relevant to the times. Members were chosen from various backgrounds, professional and religious; the legal profession was well represented by several senior lawyers including seven Senior Advocates of Nigeria, a Judge of the Court of Appeal and several other judges.

The Review proceeded professionally and amicably but there were a few areas that generated a great deal of passion. One in particular was Section 10 of the 1979 Constitution which states that no religion should be adopted as a state religion. "The session was highly tense and eventually we had to adjourn to reconvene after a long weekend," no doubt to allow tempers to calm and to give room for further thought. The female delegates worked well together but some really heated arguments went on between the male delegates. When sensitive matters came up for discussion those delegates who did not attend as conscientiously as Fati clearly did, would turn up to weigh in on their side of the debate. At the conclusion of the Review, the Chairman read a prepared statement to the press and the report was duly submitted to the Government of the day. It was notable that during the period of consultation and debate none of the members spoke to the press and neither did they leak information on the sessions which were held in strict confidence. This is very different from the most recently concluded Constitutional Conference which was conducted in the full glare of the press with delegates using the media to "press" their points.

At the conclusion of the Constitution Review, a Constituent Assembly was convened for which Fati was nominated. "This experience was completely different. After the President had addressed the delegates we had a whole month of sitting where not much work was done." The Chairman set the tone and from their comments it appeared that many of the delegates had not even bothered to read the Constitution. Delegates did not take full advantage of the working papers made available to them and there was much posturing and playing to the gallery. Fati says with regret that by making extreme statements demanding new constitutional provisions for which the Constitution already provided, the delegates caused much damage to inter regional relationships. The activities of these delegates further "polarised" the country. "There was so much rancour on issues of religion and ethnicity" that it was not a pleasant experience, but, she says with finality, "I considered it part of my civic duty to Nigeria to see it through." Many of the male delegates were subsequently appointed to high flying positions and although many of the women delegates were in her opinion more competent, they have not had the same success.

WRAPA

Her husband's career in the Nigerian Army inevitably meant that she was involved in duties outside her own career as a lawyer. After the sudden death of General Sanni Abacha, the unelected Head of State, her husband, who had risen to become General Abubakar, was called upon to oversee and effect the transition from military dictatorship to democratically elected government. While he was engaged on this important work, Fati set up WRAPA (the Women's Rights Advancement and Protection Alternative) as a movement for women to find a way of resolving those issues that "we as women always complain about, but also do nothing about." She had long had an interest in women's rights and at the Fourth World Conference on women in Beijing in 1995, which she attended as an observer, she was struck by the progress women had made in some countries simply by organising themselves into a cohesive group to deal with injustices that had previously seemed intractable. She attended various sub committee groups and listened carefully to the representatives of various Non-governmental Organisations as well as attending government discussion forums.

"Women did talk about the problems they were facing but more importantly they also talked about how they went about providing solutions to these problems." The Beijing Conference made a lasting impression and when the time came, Fati wasted no time in seizing the opportunity to make a positive difference in her own country. Fati relied heavily on the advice of Professor Jadesola Akande, a veteran of the NGO movement, because she felt that if the new charity was to be sustainable after the period of her husband's service to the nation as Head of State had ended, it must remain entirely separate from the Government. She succeeded on both counts as over seven years later WRAPA has gone from strength to strength in helping countless women including Amina Lawal, who was the unfortunate subject of the notorious adultery case that made headlines around the world at the time. However, despite all the international publicity interest the world's media remained strangely unaware of WRAPA's involvement.

The reality is that if it had not been for WRAPA's intervention, Amina Lawal would probably have been stoned to death. In the first place it was WRAPA volunteers who ensured that the appeal was filed within the time allowed by the Sharia Court. WRAPA also instructed Counsel, a kindly man who had helped on other occasions and who generously gave up his time and resources to prepare the nine grounds on which the Appeal was pursued and eventually won. He remained lead counsel even when publicity drew others to involvement in the case, persisted in his determined pursuit of the case and did not relent until the sentence was over turned.

But this is not the only success of the organisation which Fati founded to promote the legal, human, social and natural rights of women. She herself uses her undoubted advocacy skills to promote understanding of the difficulties faced by women when oppressed by severe traditional practices and domestic violence. WRAPA now has a network in 36 states and has helped to provide legal aid and counselling to more than 2,500 women, and she herself is an indefatigable writer for the WRAPA Newsletter.

Final accolade

The most appropriate summary of her legal character and career comes from the citation in support of her Honorary Degree at her alma mater, where it was said that her opinions are widely regarded by her peers as "reflecting sound reasoning familiar to practising lawyers and legal scholars. Your opinions not merely explain, they educate and elucidate. They are marked by clarity and elegance. You believe that the highest duty of the legal system is to serve the ends of justice."

Funke Adekoya

*Funke Adekoya is the Managing Partner of AELEX Legal
Practitioners and Arbitrators with offices in Lagos, Port Harcourt
and Accra. She is one of only 5 women who are Senior Advocates
of Nigeria. She is a current Vice President of the Nigerian Bar
Association.*

Although Funke Adekoya is Nigerian she was born in
Birmingham, England, where her father was studying
Law at the time. The family returned to Nigeria
when she was ten years old, but it was not until they arrived
that she and her siblings discovered that the 'holiday' they
had eagerly anticipated would be permanent and that Funke
would not be returning to the primary school she had
attended in London.

Her secondary school career began in Lagos at Our Lady of
Apostles where she acquitted herself creditably, followed by
St Anne's Ibadan where she studied for A Levels. By her own
admission she had begun to take her studies far less seriously
with the result that she did not make the required grades. In
the Principal's opinion she had been much too young when
she sat her A Levels and he advised that she should repeat a
year and re-take them. It was at this point that Funke showed
the rebellious nature that has stood her in good stead and
her father showed his wisdom in knowing how to deal with

his headstrong daughter. Funke refused point blank to return to a school which she did not like, and where she would have felt demoted and demotivated by being placed in the class beneath the one in which she had been studying.

Housework and teaching

After a brief but futile attempt to change her mind Funke's father said matter of factly, "Well fine, as you make your bed so shall you lie on it. If you do not want to go back you do not have to go back."

So the teenage Funke left Lagos to join her father in Makurdi where he was at that time working as a magistrate in Benue Magistrates Court. "I learned how to cook, clean and keep house. I also found a job as a school teacher." When her father was transferred to Oturkpo (a smaller town, also in Benue State) she found a job in St Anne's School, Oturkpo. After about nine months of this harsh reality, she realised that perhaps school was the lesser evil and applied for the preliminary course in Law at the University of Ife, an alternative way of gaining entry to a degree course from the standard A Level route. As soon as she was given a place she returned to school without any further fuss, and now feels that the academic year spent out of school actually benefited her, because when she returned, she took her studies extremely seriously.

Next steps

Funke found that she was the youngest but one in her set at the Law Faculty and she remembers with a slightly mischievous smile that, "the poor chap who was younger than me by about six months, I am sure will never forget it." She finished with an Upper Second Class Degree, although "I was not quite sure of the significance of these classifications at the time." As she had also received three Faculty prizes there were discussions between the lecturers as to whether she had actually achieved her full potential in the examinations and whether she should have been awarded a First Class Honours Degree instead. But the Upper Second stood.

Now Funke had a life plan. First she would complete her legal studies at Law School in Lagos, then she would return to the University of Ife to serve her compulsory National Youth Service Corps (NYSC) year with the Law Faculty as a graduate assistant in the hope that she would be retained as a full lecturer. This was a particularly attractive option because it would have meant that the University would later fund her professional development if she chose to enrol for a Masters Degree in Law. However, her lecturers at Ife, who had taken a special interest in her progress and future career, advised her to "go out there" and serve the NYSC in whatever capacity she was deployed. After that she could return to teach in the Faculty with a wider experience of life in general. They encouraged her to work hard and to maintain good grades and assured her that after Law School and her NYSC year there would be a position for her in the Law Faculty. This she felt was an honour as it was not an opportunity made available to all students.

Into private practice

But life took another and slightly unexpected turn.

NYSC posted her to the private sector Law firm of Abdullahi & Co in Kaduna, and the rest as they say is history. "That was it. I just never went back to teaching. It opened a whole new vista and I found I enjoyed practice immensely." She did eventually study for a Masters Degree in Law but it was at Harvard University in the United States following which "I returned to practice, still in the private sector and I have been in private practice ever since." Perhaps, if her lecturers had not dissuaded her from serving the NYSC in the Ife Law Faculty as she had originally planned, she would have followed an entirely different career path and "would very probably not have been where I am today." Who knows, as all those lecturers who encouraged her are now in private practice and are all also Senior Advocates of Nigeria. What is important, and says a lot about Funke's character and attitude to life, is that she saw something in private practice that attracted her, and she grasped the opportunity to pursue it.

Why Law?

Funke had never seriously considered any other profession as a career. Law was part of the household experience, and both she and her sister ended up studying Law. "When we were young, my father was reading Law books and we were always around when he was studying and later writing judgements, so we never really thought of anything else. In the evenings when we were sent to bed we used to play at being in the court, taking the parts of the judge and the jury. I really never gave it much thought because I had always, always known that this was what I would do." The only other possibility that crossed her mind in any serious way was acting. Throughout her time at University she was a member of the University Drama Group during term time and during the holidays worked at NTA (the Nigeria Television Authority).

Funke also acted on television and her fantasy ambition was to combine the two careers of lawyer and actress. "But I was told categorically that I could not be a lawyer and an actress at the same time." When she argued that Francesca

Emanuel, a woman Permanent Secretary in Nigeria, also had a singing career, Funke was told that she was an opera singer. It was nonetheless still not acceptable to combine opera singing with the Law. "I was also told that the legal profession did not take kindly to such antics and that it would be unbefitting."

Funke did not rediscover her acting talent until she became an advocate in the Courts of Justice. "When you are standing in a Court before a judge, there is an element of play acting in the process of advocating your client's case." To some extent therefore Funke was able to achieve a substantial part of what she originally wanted. She stayed in private practice with Abdullahi & Co, took one day at a time and just kept on going.

To America

At the end of her NYSC stint with Abdullahi & Co, Funke applied to three Ivy League Universities in the United States for admission into their Masters programmes. This was an unusual choice as American Law Schools were not popular with Nigerian lawyers at that time. Perhaps because of the link with University College, Ibadan, which was part of the University of London, everyone wanted to go to England, and mainly to University of London colleges, such as the School of African and Oriental Studies and University College, London.

Yale, which was her first choice, turned her down, Columbia gave her a place and no funding but Harvard offered her not only a place but also a scholarship. It was therefore no contest as to which University got her vote! She admits that she really did not know very much about American Law Schools, but that what she was sure of was that she did not want to return to England which she had already lived in as a child because she had a very strong desire to experience "something new."

Her decision about which American universities to approach was informed more by speaking to friends and family rather than by rigorous research. From them she gathered that Yale, Columbia and Harvard were the universities most favoured by Nigerians, and that Yale was regarded as "the place to go." However, her disappointment at not getting in there was soon over when she realised just how prestigious and highly regarded was Harvard, her third choice university, both in the United States and the rest of the world. But, she points out, in Nigeria of the Seventies, there was little awareness, and certainly not to the level there is now of the relative standing of international universities. Perhaps it was as well that she did not realise at the time just how much competition there was for places at Yale, Columbia and Harvard, although it seems unlikely that knowledge of the potential competition would have deterred Funke from seeking a place at the college of her choice.

Returning from America

Unusually Funke was attracted by both Corporate and Family Law. Both areas of Law she saw as being concerned with the regulation of relationships within defined legal entities. "The concept of a family is similar to that of a corporation, only that the latter is in general a larger and more public entity." It was only on her return to Nigeria that she discovered that there was a dichotomy between 'soft' law and 'hard' law and the specialist LLM courses she had chosen (in Securities, Mergers and Monopolies) all seemed to be in hard Law subjects.

The return to her future professional life was also a return to Kaduna and Abdullahi and Co, where she soon had the opportunity of putting the knowledge gained at Harvard into practice, as a large portion of the work in her firm involved debentures, trust entities, regulation issues and other corporate law matters.

Making the adjustment from the intellectual challenge of a completely different culture to life back in traditional Kaduna was not too difficult. Even though the North is commonly regarded as more conservative than the South, Funke feels that "I was not treated any differently at Abdullahi and Co because I was a woman. Indeed I enjoyed my time there immensely, I liked the Northern part of Nigeria very much and felt at home there."

This is not to say that there were not one or two little local difficulties. One day the Alhaji for whom she had been conducting a matter, came into Chambers to discuss it. "But when he realised that a woman was dealing with it, he went to tell my boss that this was not acceptable." Funke was called into her boss's office to be asked whether she knew the client. "Yes," she replied, "I am dealing with his debt recovery matter which is coming up for hearing next week, and he has come in for a meeting in order to prepare for the hearing and then asked to see you."

Funke's boss then called for the Alhaji's file and told Funke that "he does not want you to be his lawyer so I am giving him his file and asking him to leave as the firm cannot continue to act for him." The Alhaji broke into a torrent of Hausa (the Nigerian language predominantly spoken in the North). As Funke did not understand what he said she could only look on incredulously. But she did realise from his manner that the man was very apologetic "and eventually my boss was mollified." Later that evening she was told that the Alhaji had come to complain that he did not want a woman handling his matter, and despite being assured by

Funke's boss that he as her principal had every confidence in her abilities as a lawyer, the man was adamant that her boss deal with the situation decisively once and for all. Which was exactly what Funke's boss did, although not as the Alhaji had anticipated.

Reality strikes

As well as a practical legal training Funke also gained a husband in Kaduna, and when he was posted to Lagos she went with him.

She describes the move to Lagos as a great shock to the system. With all the hustle and bustle and competition amongst lawyers, "it was like moving from a nice slow pond to a river, a fast flowing river. There was really this urge to prove one's self." At the time that she told her boss in Kaduna that she was moving to Lagos with her husband he had asked her to open a branch office for Abdullahi & Co in Lagos as this had been an ambition which he had considered but had not previously pursued because he had not found the right person to assist him. "I turned it down as I wanted to go out into the big wide world."

However, after three months working for another firm in Lagos she called her boss to ask whether the offer was still open. "Fortunately it was and I quickly handed in my resignation and returned to familiar territory where I was looked at as a person and judged for my abilities rather than being seen only as a female."

From this period of her life in Lagos there is one thing that she feels she learned and values particularly highly. That is good time management. "This is so crucial to the successful and effective pursuit of your career aspirations. I say this time and again to the women lawyers coming after me. You must learn to manage your time if you want to compete with the men, particularly if you have a family and a home to organise as well." For many years Funke kept a humble t-shirt because it had emblazoned on it words which summed up the situation of working women so aptly. It read "to be a career woman you have to look like a woman, act like a man and work like a dog."

"You had to do one and a half times as much work as a man just to put the same amount the man was putting on the table." But simultaneously women had to live with the humiliating assumption that they simply would not perform to the level of their male colleagues, and would not be prepared to put in the hours to be able to do so. Towards closing time she would receive comments such as "Are you still here?" or "You haven't gone home?" said with mock concern. "Well of course I am still here," she would reply yet again, "it's not closing time yet." If she had chosen to take advantage of these suggestions it would paradoxically have been acceptable as she was regarded as "only a woman after all" who was not expected to stay the course.

Funke knows that she has a reputation in some quarters for being "pushy, aggressive and very unfeminine but it does not bother me one bit. I do not see what my gender has to do with my work and I am a litigator, so it is about going out there and being the best advocate possible."

Male and female law

After 13 years Funke set up in practice on her own "and that was when I found out that there were areas of practice generally seen as 'feminine.' and that women were not expected to practise in my area of expertise." Women lawyers she discovered were usually probate lawyers, divorce lawyers or trust lawyers, and everyone assumed that she was a specialist in one of those areas. In America she had not realised that the Corporate Law subjects she had studied were in Nigeria considered "reserved for men".

When Funke began her legal career this was probably not surprising. She was for example one of only the second set of women lawyers to serve on the NYSC scheme. "We had heard all these horror stories about the first set of women to be posted out, how they had wept in court and been bullied by colleagues. In a nutshell the impression was that they could not hold their own and reacted in very feminine ways under pressure by bursting into tears." The magistrates were waiting for Funke and her young female colleagues and anticipated "much more fun along those lines, but we were determined not to give an inch."

"The mentality was, here comes another set of women, we are going to make them cry and we are going to harass them." However, forewarned is forearmed, and every one of the group of seven young women was determined that what had happened to their predecessors would not happen to them. They resolved that none of them would break down under pressure and that no matter what was thrown at them they would not burst into tears - at least not publicly. Funke confesses that in many ways they actually enjoyed it. "We were given no quarter, we expected none and just got on with it." There were certain difficulties about operating in the predominantly Muslim Northern part of the country, but Funke and her fellow corpers did not feel that it was an imposition to observe the norms of the community in which they lived and worked, to recognise that as women there were certain places they could not enter, and that they must be careful about the way that they dressed when not in regulation NYSC gear. When on occasion an archetypal elderly magistrate would peer over his spectacles and refer to Funke as "my dear" she simply "ignored such behaviour and rose above it."

The toughness that was produced by this treatment stood her in good stead when she became more senior and her firm grew and took on younger lawyers. Some of them made the foolish mistake of assuming that they could get away with "coming in late to-day and leaving early to-morrow" just because she was a woman and would not enforce discipline. And then "immediately you put your foot down, you were seen as unfeminine by subordinates as well. Those were the days of Margaret Thatcher in the United Kingdom and I was called The Iron Lady behind my back and eventually to my face."

Balancing work and home life

In Nigeria as in other countries there is a special problem for working mothers. How does a woman keep the balance between her professional responsibilities and her duty to her family? "I was very lucky and I think most African women professionals are very lucky in that we have our indigenous social security system, which is the extended family." Although Funke believes that this has to some extent broken down now, when she was younger it was still very much in existence. "I had a mother in law who lived two streets away from me who was an absolute marvel, so that my kids came home from school and stayed with her until I got home."

Very early on in her time in Lagos Funke took an important decision which also improved her productivity. "You have a choice, you drive yourself and ruin your body or you get a driver and ruin your car. I opted for the latter and soon became very adept at working in the car. I can work anywhere. Traffic jams do not bother me as I can utilise the time to read my briefs. I also gave my driver strict instructions that wherever I was at half past one in the afternoon, he should leave immediately and go to pick my children up from school. Often I would come out of Court to find that my driver had gone on the school run. As there were no 'okadas' (motorcycle taxis) then I did my fair share of hopping on taxis and buses including the usually decrepit and overcrowded mammy wagons called 'molues' to get me to my next appointment."

By rigorous organisation Funke usually managed to keep her family and professional lives separate, but inevitably there could be the occasional overlap. On one occasion she had promised to be at the school Open Day of one of her children. Unfortunately she was in Court, matters dragged on and at twelve thirty she politely requested an adjournment. The Judge replied that "we could certainly carry on since he was prepared to and we were right in the flow of things." Funke "made all the usual excuses, the things that men say and get away with" but the Judge would have none of it. "Eventually I had to come clean and tell him that I had made a promise to my child expecting that we would conclude at the usual time from court. He was very understanding and granted the adjournment. That was the one and only time I had to say in Court that I wanted an adjournment because I had home issues and fortunately the judge was very accommodating and said well, you have been on your feet since nine o'clock, so off you go and the matter was adjourned."

Even more organisation

In order to succeed a woman needs "family support and time management skills and to be adaptable. I am adept at working in the car where I can draft, I can read and I can do any other work that I would normally undertake in the office." Funke makes it clear to younger female lawyers "that you just have to make every minute count. You also have to decide early on what is important in your life and what is not. The problem of the working woman is that she does not realise that not everything worth doing is worth doing well." This has meant that Funke has had to make some hard if only temporary choices. For many years she did not visit friends who did not have children; her week-ends were devoted to her children and she did not want to take any of this time away from them.

She chose to spend time with those friends who were also bringing up young families, so that she could combine seeing them with encouraging her children's social lives. It also meant that there was a readymade network of support. "It was not that I deliberately cut out friends who were single, but somehow they got shifted to the backburner at that period in time and if they were good friends they understood. Saturdays were for my kids and if you are going to be upset because my kids are jumping all over your sofa then we will maintain our friendship by telephone. So basically time management was the key. You have to know what is important to you and weed out what is not."

A typical day for Funke now starts at about 6.00 am and she arrives at the office about 7.00 am to begin an hour spent sorting out emails and post. This is followed by a morning in Court until about noon when she returns to the office to deal with her administrative issues as managing partner and to supervise her juniors in the Litigation Department which is still her responsibility. After such a long twelve hour day she relaxes by going to parties when she has the opportunity "and I have since discovered that on Sunday mornings there are very good movies on TV so I watch those and read a good book when I can find one."

The latter activities are important because despite her devotion to her family and her dedication to work, Funke insists that there must also be "your own personal space outside of work and family. For me, it was my Lion's Club and church activities. You must have something that is just yours."

Let's talk about AELEX

For a partnership to succeed it must have elements of common experience and also a common philosophy. All five founding partners of AELEX achieved their second degrees in the United States. All of them also had a good idea about what is involved in working for and with foreign law international firms and how they are run. "I think that made things easier." They were all sole practitioners burdened with overwork and insufficient support. "You go away for two weeks and when you return you cannot talk to anyone for another four weeks as you return to a table piled high with work in progress."

They started talking about the concept of some sort of working together in 1999. "Soji Owubade and I broached the idea to others that we might form an alliance of specialist law firms in Nigeria who would cross refer work to each other. We started meeting to discuss the modalities of implementation over lunch, and at that point we were going to call it the Law Firm Alliance." As so often with busy people they found it relatively easy to settle on action points but then the action points did not move forward very speedily.

After a while, when they realised that they had agreed only on who would be the main players and what would be the specialist areas that they would concentrate on, they changed tack. They asked themselves whether engaging in joint marketing, joint websites, and roadshows and perhaps even setting up a central telephone service which would direct potential clients to the appropriate firm was all that they really needed.

After two years of this talking and bouncing ideas back and forth without further progress, "Soji suggested that we get married so to speak, instead of this loose arrangement of, as he put it, flirting with each other or even an engagement." He had realised that no one really wanted an alliance because there was no way of enforcing reciprocity. Potentially one alliance member might refer work to another alliance member who would say thank you, but would then retain subsequent work that should really be referred to other specialist members of the alliance. In Soji's view the best plan would be to merge the individual firms and to take it from there.

The big questions

This left them with the big question of "can we work together and do we share the same ethics and attitude to work?"

They very soon found that they had sufficient common ground to make the venture worthwhile. One fundamental premise was that "our main interest was law practice, not law combined with another career such as commerce or politics as is so common these days, and we wanted to build and leave behind a legacy in this profession as well as to earn a decent living from practice." After agreeing that the firm should not be known by the name of one or other of a set of individuals, "we made overtures to a branding company who quoted us an astronomical sum which we simply could not afford. We then got together one Saturday and said that we would not rise from the meeting until we had a name for the firm, and so we all started throwing around ideas until eventually we arrived at our name."

Once they got beyond this point the challenges for each of them were multiple, but as Funke points out the feeling of loss of independence should not be underestimated. "You are no longer your own boss. Other people's financial wellbeing is dependent on you, so you cannot just disappear and not come to work. You have to be prepared to give up some power and decision making. As a sole practitioner, you run your own show, fire as you like and hire as you like, but in partnership you have to consult and accept the majority decision even where it is not what you yourself want. As the only female amongst four men, I feel like I know first hand what polyandry is all about as I have had to balance and stabilise the relationships within the firm to a certain extent."

However the advantages have far outweighed whatever disadvantages or challenges there have been "and it has been worth it. I would recommend this route to growth for anyone in private practice, because it gives the opportunity to cross sell and deal with clients as a one stop shop. It is the only way to grow and to compete internationally."

Learning and recognition

Funke was delighted and felt highly honoured when she was elevated to the position of Senior Advocate of Nigeria (SAN). "This is because it is like getting to Form Five, there is not much more you can do after that, except if you want to go into the Judiciary which I have no interest in doing. It is an acknowledgement from the profession that you are a leader and considered fit to be a role model and an example." Only six women have ever been awarded the accolade of SAN in the whole history of Nigeria of whom five (Phoebe Ajayi-Obe, Justina Offiah, Folake Solanke, Abimbola Williams and of course Funke) are alive today. In total only about 270 SAN have ever been appointed, so it is a rare honour and privilege and for Funke it has been "the high point of my career."

Her pragmatic and positive approach to life has stood her in good stead in the face of difficulties. She takes the attitude that whatever has happened to her during her life has been an opportunity for her to learn something. "These lessons have served me well so I do not regret anything."

As to the position of women in to-day's society and in the Law in particular, Funke believes very firmly that there is no profession that should be patronisingly designated as "suitable for women." Women should go into whatever profession they choose. The question of 'suitability' should arise only in terms of individual characteristics. Thus if someone is impatient by nature, then perhaps Law might not be suitable, but that she points out "has nothing to do with your gender. If there are any special skills that women have that perhaps men generally do not have, it is probably a sense of intuition to read beyond the words when dealing with a client. And to be successful in the Law, you must also have a passion for people. You have to love what you are doing."

Advice to young lawyers

Funke has a continuing concern about practice standards. "I think lawyers could give a better quality of service," but she takes a historical perspective on this. "We are at a point of transition. The previous generation practised law as a vocation and because there were so few of them, they were able to earn a decent living from it. Now we have a proliferation of lawyers, and we need to understand that Law is not just a vocation but a business as well." It is essential that lawyers understand that both aspects are important. They also need to be able to make sure that their clients understand what providing a quality service involves and that they will have to pay a premium for it. "Until we do that, standards will continue to fall."

Funke believes in this so passionately that she currently chairs the committee reviewing the curriculum for both the Law School and the universities, "so that by the time we finish, the lawyers that will be trained thereafter will hit the ground running."

She is also quite clear that entering the Law is not a get rich quick scheme. "If you are entering into legal practice, do not expect to make a lot of money in the first five years. Whatever little you are paid, reinvest it in your professional development and in building up the resources that you need to maintain your practice." She emphasises the importance of "looking the part" to give the impression of success and gravitas that will attract new clients. The assistance that young lawyers could obtain from family and friends in building a practice should also not be ignored. They can spread the word about a young lawyer's competence until the point where a justified good reputation has been built up which in itself would bring in new work.

Summing up

Asking Funke to consider her life so far is almost like asking for a judicial summary as she says calmly and thoughtfully that "I would not change anything and I would certainly not consider another profession." What she says reflects her very measured attitude to the position of women in society as well as women in the legal profession, and is therefore very much worth listening to. It is about the choices that we make and how we live with them and move forward. "The things that did not meet my expectation, such as the proverbial glass ceiling, I would have encountered in other professions as well."

"Yes, I had to deal with issues such as how to balance my home and children with my work life, and in the balancing process perhaps I did slow down in comparison to what men in my shoes might have achieved, but I would still not have given up my family life for anything because for me that is the most important thing and my husband and children come first. So I would not change anything."

Sena Anthony

Sena Anthony is Group General Manager, Corporate Secretariat and Legal Division and Secretary to the Corporation of the Nigerian National Petroleum Company (NNPC), the first woman to be appointed to such a post in the company.

Sena Anthony, or Yeye Olofin as she could alternatively be called for she is a traditional Lagos Chief, began her legal career in 1974 with the Federal Ministry of Justice. Four years later the University of Lagos graduate made the move from Government lawyer to corporate employee. Having therefore spent almost thirty years with the same company experiencing in-house positions from the most junior to the most senior, she is in a good position to comment on the reasons for working in-house.

Sena does not consider that there was any one thing which informed her decision to apply for a position as in-house counsel. She started from a belief that there is no wrong or right path in terms of a career in the law, because there are many avenues down which one can go and many times that one can opt for another path. "I think it's just probably a sequence of events that leads you to where you end up. At the end of the day, it's a personal decision, whether you want to have your own chambers or whether you want to work in an organisation as an in-house counsel." One thing is certain, which is that for Sena life as an in-house lawyer is certainly not second best.

Industry expert

Sena has been with NNPC since 1978 so it would be easy to pigeon-hole her as a specialist solely in Oil and Gas Law. "No, that's a mistake that people make. As an in-house counsel, you have to be an expert in everything. In an organisation like NNPC we're not just into Oil and Gas; we're into all the support services, whether they are upstream or downstream. So any in-house counsel has to have the capability of supervising litigation and also property transactions. You may think that they are unrelated, but if the company acquires property, all sorts of litigation situations could arise, perhaps in respect of pollution or breach of contract. So you'll find that in-house counsel are like general medical practitioners in that they need to have a knowledge of all the different areas of Law."

Sena points out that an oil and gas company will own or lease all sorts of hardware, such as a fleet of helicopters and air craft as well as the obvious things like offshore installations, pipelines and tankers. The company will also have to enter into agreements with Government for exploration licences and with landowners and contractors in order to acquire land for and build administrative buildings, storage depots and facilities for its workers. The amount and type of Law involved in all these transactions and agreements is substantial. "We really have to have a knowledge of everything. We need to know about Aviation Law and the Law relating to Goods and Services; as in-house lawyers we really have to have a broad base of legal knowledge."

She goes on to point out that being in charge of the NNPC Legal Division means that she herself must also "know everything" or at least sufficient of everything in order to supervise her legal staff effectively. Despite her implicit statement that in-house counsel need to be Jacks and Jills of All Trades Sena's own expertise in her primary field of Oil and Gas Law is so well regarded that she became the first woman and the first African to chair the IBA Section on Energy and Natural Resources.

A career in the Law?

Sena has no doubt in her own mind that she made the right choice in switching from Governmental work to corporate work, and even less doubt about her decision to become a lawyer in the first place. Any statements about her own career and her own decisions come from a woman who is organised and definite in her opinions, but she feels that whether or not a young person should become a lawyer is entirely a matter of personal choice. She would hesitate to persuade someone of the merit of Law as a career, probably because she would feel that someone who was considering such a career should be able to research its possibilities and to make up her own mind. "It is very much a matter of personal choice. And once you have decided, it's another matter of choice whether you are going to be a barrister going to court, or are going to work in Government or become an in-house counsel." As many large Nigerian Chambers have developed specialist arms devoted solely to Commercial Law work, it is now possible to pursue this specialism without actually being actively engaged in business. This means that these chambers are just as focused on the contractual and the advisory as on the litigation side of things. Sena is a large consumer of the work of these chambers and is therefore in an excellent position to observe any changes in the balance of their work and interest. And she sees this as an opportunity for young lawyers. "So it depends really. It's like asking a young graduate, would you like to be a solicitor or a barrister, it's really a personal choice."

Becoming an in-house lawyer

On the other hand Sena is able to give sound practical advice to young people seeking their first position as in-house lawyers. "Well, of course they have to apply to a company to take them." This may seem a very obvious point to make until Sena observes that in some cases applying may simply be a waste of time. "A lot of the companies are looking for somebody with enough experience to be able to come aboard and do the work immediately. You'll find that there are a lot of junior lawyers trying to get into companies, even though they don't have experience and very few companies actually take young lawyers." Companies in fact prefer lawyers to have undergone the first stages of their legal career by working in chambers or in an institution such as a Ministry, working for the Government. The first years of a young lawyer's career are spent simply becoming familiar with office and court procedures, drafting and correspondence, making sound arguments and learning to be comfortable with clients and other lawyers. It is clear that companies do not expect to have to train their new recruits in matters other than those which are most relevant to their own business.

"Because a lot of the things we do are concerned with due diligence and compliance documents, and complying with regulations, you'll find that a lot of companies actually consider lawyers who have worked in Government very attractive. Companies will anticipate that they will usually have a working knowledge of what the relevant Laws are, which the new lawyers can then interpret for them to ensure that the companies are regulatorily compliant." Sena comments that there are a lot of young lawyers who actually avoid going to work for Government, which is not in fact a good career decision for someone who has the ambition to be an in-house lawyer. "In many ways working for Government is actually the basis of being an in-house counsel. The truth of the matter is that lawyers who work for Government are actually in-house counsel to Government."

Women as in-house counsel

A person's competence and ambition are far more important to Sena than gender. Consequently she is not a member of any women's networking groups. "I don't believe in it. The world consists of men and women." The fact of her being female had no obvious impact on her own decision to be a lawyer, for as she says with simple certainly, "I have always known that I wanted to be a lawyer, I like reading."

She is far more concerned that young people go in-house for the right reasons. In her view being an in-house counsel requires a certain sort of character. "You have to be able to take satisfaction from making a good job of what you are doing. If you're aggressively looking for money, and I notice that a lot of young people nowadays are overly-focused on looking for a large income, you won't find it by being an in-house counsel" Being able to be content with having done a job well rather than requiring massive financial rewards is perhaps one of the reasons that a lot of women do go in-house. "So, its one of the things you have to ask yourself. Do you want to be within the shortest possible time earning a lot, making tons of money? Because if that is it, your career path shouldn't be that of a lawyer."

Having participated in many conferences internationally, being a member of the Nominations Committee of the International Bar Association and a member of the LNG Committee of the Association of International Petroleum Negotiators she has been in the position to observe the financial development of law firms in many other countries. "You can find a lot of rich and successful lawyers in many of the firms in London, where you can make partnership quickly, and if you're in one of the top City firms and you're a partner, you're going to get to the millions of pounds very quickly. Similarly in the US, if you're prepared to work round the clock as a lawyer, you're going to get the millions very quickly."

Success in Nigeria

Increasing globalisation and the development of Nigerian industry and natural resource exploitation has required the development of a different sort of Nigerian law firm, one whose lawyers acquire an increasing expertise in international law and have the ability to negotiate with foreign companies. "We now have some very successful legal firms in Nigeria with partners who are rich. It's beginning to happen in Nigeria as well because the privatisation exercise has created a lot of large legal work." Sena views the wealth of legal firms as a positive sign of Nigeria's potential prosperity and stability, an encouraging sign for someone who is devoutly involved with her church and is the Patron of the Boys and Girls Brigade of the Holy Cross Cathedral in Lagos. "Because of the success of our transition to democracy, we are now a very attractive country for third party financing. So this has meant that many lawyers have gone into Project Finance, and as they are being paid in dollars they tend to get rich very quickly."

"But at the end of the day, you'll find that as a lawyer, money isn't everything. It is job satisfaction, the sense that it is the actual work that you are doing and the positive impact you're making within the profession that really gives you joy rather than being vastly well remunerated."

Despite the international and corporate focus of her work, Sena still retains a sense that the role of the lawyer is to serve her community, in her case her colleagues at NNPC as individuals. She regards it not as a chore but almost as an accolade that her colleagues come to her for advice on their personal legal issues. This she considers to be "a great satisfaction. They come for all sorts of things. They come for advice on drafting wills, and every so often, one of my lawyers just sends round an article on Will drafting addressing the questions that people should be considering. So we actually do assist on a personal level as well as at corporate level, sometimes with personal documentation and things like that." This is not something that is part of Sena's job description. "It's absolutely voluntary." And simply confirms what she said before, about money not being everything.

Uju Aisha Hassan Baba

Uju Aisha Hassan Baba is the Director General of the Legal Aid Council

Along with a myriad other Government Departments the Legal Aid Council has its headquarters in a sprawling building in Abuja. Despite the size of the building and the number of people working from the building, conservatively about a thousand, it is very easy to find Mrs Hassan Baba as workers' faces light up in recognition when asked for the way to her office. "DG" (shorthand for Director General) is not some faceless figure to the people who work for her, but someone who has won their trust and admiration. In the warren of offices all know where DG's office can be found.

Aisha works in a small unpretentious office and from behind a proportionately small and functional desk she beams with surprisingly youthful candour. Speaking with an unexpected English accent, she responds to questions frankly and at times in refreshingly blunt language. If there is an important point to be made Aisha feels no need to adopt the usual diplomacy and tact of Nigerian speech.

The reluctant lawyer

As Shakespeare said, some have greatness thrust upon them, and Aisha would not have been sitting behind her small desk with a very large remit to provide legal assistance to the less fortunate if it had not been for her grandmother who insisted that she return from England to undertake professional education. Aisha wanted to be an artist, but her family gave her only the choice of which profession she was to follow. They left her in no doubt that the chancy life of an artist was not for her. Aisha therefore applied for a place in the Faculty of Law.

"When I was admitted I went along to the lectures, but really I had no interest in the subject and did the minimum amount of work that I could get away with throughout my time at University." Following her graduation from the University of Nigeria, Nsukka, she attended the Nigerian Law School and was called to the Bar, before working for the Ministry of Justice as a prosecutor during her National Service year. Even after this was completed she remained with the Ministry of Justice and continued to pursue her prosecutions with the utmost zeal "because I am naturally a very hard worker, but it was about four years before I realised that Law really was my calling." This discovery probably coincided with the point in her prosecution career where she had honed her advocacy skills sufficiently that she could begin to enjoy achieving court-room results. "As I was a prosecutor, I had to win the case and that was all that mattered." This attitude meant that she rarely lost. "I was very good in court – people told me. I was a very good prosecutor."

Volte face

When in 1999 Aisha was appointed to head the Legal Aid Council, she found herself on the other side of the fence. "The prosecutor in me was still working and I found it very hard to change my psyche to do the job of a Public Defender properly, let alone be the Chief Public Defender, which is where I have found myself. It was very hard and it took me some time to adjust." Aisha also found the Council a disheartening place in which to work; it had been set up by the military as the result of a 1976 Decree and there had very little improvement from then until Aisha's appointment in 1999. "The place was dead, and having come from a background as a prosecutor I just did not know where to start. For the first two years, it was hard to find direction until I started my prison visits. Then I stopped seeing people as cases, and realised that they were human beings. They were human beings with problems and lives of their own, some of them children – dysfunctional children – and people that exist on the fringes of society that most Nigerians cannot imagine exist in our country to-day. That was when I found direction and began to really work to re-organise the system and the structures." And that was when Aisha coined the mission statement which drives her organisation – "Giving voice to the voiceless."

Aisha says that from this point, it suddenly became very easy to see people as clients and not as cases and to relate to their difficulties. "And I stopped being moralistic or judgemental. The fact of their poverty entitles people to free legal services and we have to provide services regardless of what someone has been accused of or what the facts are."

Every few days Aisha effectively moves her office to the prisons so that her staff can pick out the cases of the most vulnerable people, those involving children, pregnant women or women with children, the elderly or the terminally ill. These are all given attention before cases involving able bodied man, because the consequences of their being kept in difficult prison conditions are potentially so much more detrimental in the long term. "The visits also serve a very useful purpose in helping me to evaluate the conditions in which prisoners are kept awaiting trial, and how best they can be assisted in very practical ways." She speaks with pleasure of the project started by prison warders in Port Harcourt to provide education for children in the prison there. "We have been able to support this from a Legal Aid Council fund we have established for rehabilitation. Some of this support comes in the form of simple practical items such as buying pens and note books, but the Council has also assisted inmates with sewing machines and other items with which they can learn a vocational skill and through that earn a living."

Prison conditions

Aisha has been forced to learn to "switch off" after work. "To begin with I was taking work home in my mind, as I could not exorcise some of the horrendous scenes I saw on a day to day basis. My job is to defend and to secure an acquittal and I have now got to the stage where I can be totally non-judgemental and I will defend anyone, regardless of how heinous the alleged crime is said to be. It is essential that everyone has their day in Court." For Aisha, this principle cannot be compromised and indeed she speaks with missionary zeal about this being the "high point" of her career so far, because she is able to use her position to touch the lives of others in a positive way. "Every time I leave the prisons I have committed either the Council or the authorities to provide something for the prisoners. Recently we had five inmates suffering from malnutrition – one was a sixteen year old boy. What we did was to buy Complan (a nutritious cereal for babies and children) which we supplied to the prison for these inmates to ensure that they drink it twice a day to build up their bodies."

She is particularly concerned about small children who are forced to spend part of their childhood in prison because of their mothers' situation. "We have women who have been forced to keep their children in prison, because there is no state institution to take care of them, and they have no family to support and take care of the children while their mothers are in prison. So a woman has to take an 18 month old baby, or a one year old baby or a two year old baby to live with her in prison and you find that no matter how hard the prisons try, that child has to eat prison food, unless the warders contribute – and they do do that a lot. You find that the warders contribute from their private funds so that they can buy the child something special to eat or a little treat from time to time. There are two children in Benin prison for whom we provide two thousand naira a month just to ensure that they are properly fed. I see it as a privilege to be able to touch lives in this way and that is why I describe this job right now as the high point in my life. As a Muslim, and it's the same for all major religions, I believe in caring for our neighbours, and this job gives me the opportunity to do so on a daily basis."

Being a woman
One major frustration that Aisha has felt in her professional life is the attitude of certain men generally to

women in the work place. "You are not taken seriously and you have to constantly prove yourself and it is something that all women professionals have to deal with. The moment they see a woman, you almost see the look of .. 'Ah it's a woman - no challenge.'" However, she does not believe in positive discrimination in favour of women, "or putting aside slots for women because it does us no good." Aisha is certain that to progress women have to prove themselves and to earn respect for their talents. "I think now that this is less of a problem than it used to be, as people have come to realise that we are a force to be reckoned with. When we write to the Ministries perhaps in cases of wrongful dismissal for example, they take it very seriously now, not like before."

Faced with a request for advice for women aspiring to pursue a career in a profession, Aisha answers with instant but thoughtful certainty. "You must firstly believe in yourself, and your own ability to achieve the goals that you have set yourself – just as any man might." If this self belief is ingrained then women will not begin to doubt their abilities when people tell them that they cannot do something. "As far as I am concerned, there is no man who is better than me. I did not have a Godfather, and neither did I have to compromise myself to get where I am today."

At the time of her appointment to the post of DG, Aisha was at an Executive Meeting in her capacity as Attorney General of Anambra State. She was appointed by recommendation based on her past performance. "Someone remembered me and when the vacancy came up, they called me to ask if I would be interested because they had seen my performance. I did not have to lobby anyone to get this job, so I would say that the fact that you are a woman does not necessarily place you at a disadvantage if you believe in yourself." Despite her previous admission about her dilatory attitude to her university studies, she is very clear in her advice to anyone who hopes to advance in her career. "Anything that you set out to do, do it with all seriousness and dedication and you can never go wrong; it is what has stood me in good stead, people remembering how hard I work."

Mothers and work

Aisha is well aware of the opportunities that there are for women in the Twenty First Century, but also the potential difficulties of combining aspirations with traditional responsibilities. Because of women's biological make up there is an expectation that the task of nurturing a family will fall primarily on their shoulders, "but this should not interfere with your work." And her advice to women professionals is succinctly pragmatic. In essence it is that it is better to absent yourself for a while rather than be seen to fail. "If you are finding it difficult to cope, stay home until your children are less dependent and then come back to the work place to build a career. If you do not do that, you risk having a negative impact on the prospects of other women."

If employers have had a bad experience with women and now feel that they will be unreliable because their children will always be "having a toothache or a fever and she is off from work," then those employers will simply stop employing women. "I have a four year old and found myself as a Chief Executive having to deal with pregnancy and child birth. I did not want to let the side down, and I would get out of bed and get in to work regardless of how awful I felt, and my staff can testify that I probably took at the most two days off during this period. After my son was born, I was back at my desk a week later because I realised that how I dealt with this situation could impact on the next woman in my position. I made a conscious effort not to let the side down."

In order to combine work and family there will be "a lot of physical and mental sacrifices. There are times when I wake up and I do not feel like going to work but I pull myself up and I come to work because I know that they are expecting me not to come to work. Sometimes my male colleagues will come to me and say "DG, go home, why are you straining yourself" and I say to them, "I do not need to go home and I am fine thank you very much." You cannot eat the entire cake. You have to give something up, you cannot have it all. In my case what had to give was my social life. I have no social life and no leisure time, but that is the sacrifice." She did not add "that I am prepared to make," thus leaving open the suggestion that Aisha considers that this is a statement that will almost inevitably apply to all women who wish to have both professional life and a family. "And if you delegate the care of your child to a nanny or childminder or live-in maid, you must ensure that that person is well treated and happy, because they have to care for the most precious thing in your life."

Our profession

From Aisha's perspective as a public defender, the judiciary "could do better as there are simply far too many people locked up in prison awaiting trial. An accused person spends a long time in prison awaiting the trial – in hell holes, with no air conditioners and no fans because they are security risks. People are packed into tiny cells on cement floors without the most basic amenities. That is why jail breaks occur because there is so much tension and frustration. The prison congestion to my mind means that the courts are not doing well. We can do better. Lawyers could also do more. The spirit of pro bono is dead, and lawyers do not contribute to access to justice." Aisha attributes this to the pressure on lawyers to earn a decent living, "the economic factor seems to be the paramount thing," and points out that as a result the Legal Aid Council has lost over the years most of the legal practitioners who used to offer pro bono services. As she usually does when she has any opportunity to do so in her desire to bring legal help to those with no resources, she appeals for "legal practitioners to register with the Council and more importantly respond when the Council calls on them to go and defend cases. We have many lawyers registered with the Council but they do not all respond to requests to assist."

Despite all the frustrations and difficulties of acting as the figurehead for the Council and thus to some extent for the dispensation of justice for the disadvantaged, Aisha now acknowledges that her grandmother perhaps knew her better than she knew herself all those years ago. (Aisha was called to the Bar in 1981). "Twenty years down the line I am now glad that I studied law, and would not wish to do anything else." She says quietly that she gains much satisfaction from her work and enjoys the challenges and the ability to influence given by her present position. In describing why she would recommend the Law as a career, she uses the homeliest of images. "If Law is a thing, I see it as an egg – you can do so much with it. As a lawyer, there is no area you cannot have input into, and it is actually a profession particularly suited to women as it is an extension of their natural selves. To succeed in Law you have to be good at multi tasking."

Future vision

Aisha's practical solutions to the problems of prison overcrowding and child incarceration with parents are informed by a set of basic principles that she keeps in mind when she considers her role as Director General. As well as focusing on relieving "the plight of widows and under-aged children held in custody in the prisons, victims of arbitrary arrest, unlawful detention and prosecution," she has a much wider and more long-term aim in mind.

This is quite simply to "educate the ordinary Nigerians on their rights as guaranteed in Chapter IV of the 1999 Constitution and in particular what they are expected to do whenever their rights are threatened or violated by any government agency or powerful individuals in the society."

One of the initiatives that is in the process of being put in place to ensure this is the Police Duty Solicitor Scheme, which is aimed at providing basic legal advice and assistance at Police Stations for 24 hours a day, 7 days a week. This scheme will be supervised by the Legal Aid Council and in the hope that it will help to foster community policing and ensure that those accused of criminal actions are not denied access to legal advice because of their impoverished circumstances.

Summing up

Natural talent is itself not enough, whether intellectual talent or a talent for organisation. Aisha emphasises as she always does, the necessity for sheer hard work. "From the very beginning every female lawyer must be sincere and hardworking. You need to take every case seriously and you have to put all that you have into it. Without hard work, you will not succeed. I certainly would not be where I am today without working very hard. And I am proud that the people I work with always had me to fall back on when it came to the crunch."

This capacity for hard work is the only thing that Aisha extols in her own character, although even a casual observer might add courage to a list of her virtues — courage in entering the prisons that she so sincerely criticises and courage in so frequently pointing out the shortcomings of institutions in order to ameliorate the conditions of the less fortunate. That those who work with her recognise her so readily and smile at the mention of her name is also testament to her inspirational status within her field.

When reminded that she had received two national honours and international honours, she says simply that she says she felt very fulfilled and humbled that the nation had deemed it fit to honour her "little contribution" in this way.

Rahila Hadea Cudjoe

Rahila Hadea Cudjoe is the Chief Judge of Kaduna State. As well as being the first woman to hold this position, she was the first woman indigenous lawyer in Kaduna State, the first woman Legal Draftsman, the first woman Legislative Counsel and also the first woman High Court Judge in Kaduna State.

An indigene

Rahila was educated completely in Northern Nigeria. Born on 6 October 1948 in Kaduna, she attended St. Louis Primary School, Fagge, Kano, Our Lady's High School, Kaduna and Government Girls College, Dala, Kano. She obtained her LLB (Hons.) Degree at Ahmadu Bello University, Zaria, one of the original 7 Hausa city-states, and finished her professional education in 1973 at the Nigerian Law School.

Her professional career has equally been spent completely in her home state. She began as a Graduate Registrar for the then North Central State and was appointed State Counsel after being called to the Bar. She progressed to become Legal Draftsman, after specialising in Legislative Drafting and then Head of the Legal Department, Kaduna State House of Assembly. She was sworn in as a High Court Judge in 1983 and elevated to the position of Chief Judge of Kaduna State on 7 January 1997.

Personal integrity

Although such bald facts hint at her understanding of her native state, its culture, laws and government, they cannot in any way indicate the contributions that she has made both to Law and to society and the respect in which she is held. In 1992 she was chosen to head the Judicial Commission of Inquiry into the Zangon-Kataf Riots, which arose over the planned relocation of a market within the Hausa community. Her nomination to this difficult task, involving the consideration of the parts played by the various indigenous interest groups within her state suggests the high regard in which her acumen and probity were held.

In her concern that the rule of law should be paramount she is not afraid to be controversial. In her opinion "the system of funding the judiciary is a potential threat to its independence." The judiciary, especially the State High Court judiciary, has two sources of funding, from the National Judicial Council and from the State Governments. She regards this arrangement as being "very cumbersome" in its complexity, and considers that it results in the disbursement of funds to the judiciary being at times uncertain and often inadequate. If the independence of the judiciary cannot be guaranteed, then there can be no real justice.

Prisons and justice

Justice to her mind is also inadequately served if imprisonment is too readily used as a means of correction. Any upsurge of crime in society is often the result of adverse economic conditions, even if only temporary, particularly if this results in a widening of the gap between the rich and the poor, or any decline in the moral standards of society. Punishment by imprisonment is meant to correct and reform offenders. It is also meant to deter others from committing crimes. But as from all indications those objectives are not being attained, Rahila considered that "it is therefore time to look at alternatives to imprisonment. There must be an alternative to imprisonment if we are to reduce the high level of crime in our society, and improve the welfare of prisons."

If prisons are to become less congested through finding meaningful alternatives to incarceration, it is essential that the way that crimes are investigated should also be examined. This again comes down to having the resources made available, in this case to ensure that the police are properly equipped. "The police tell us that very often they have to use their own money to move around to investigate cases or to buy writing materials in order to compile their case diaries." Unfortunately it is not uncommon for the Court to be told that case diaries are missing after an accused person has spent 4-6 years awaiting trial. Believing that this sort of delay is unacceptable and does not serve justice well, she argues for the implementation of time limits within which police investigations into the culpability of an accused held on remand must be completed, failing which the accused should be discharged. Understandably the courts are rather reluctant to release those awaiting trial where serious offences have been committed. Therefore a legal limit on the time that an accused person may be held in prison awaiting trial would be a step in the right direction.

Too much sentencing

She is also highly critical of the "over-use of prison sentences by some judges." When she toured some prisons, she felt that too many cases were brought to her notice where a person who had stolen a chicken or half a bag of maize was sentenced to between 2 and 4 years' imprisonment, either with the option of a fine or even without any option of a fine. "A person who steals a chicken or half a bag of maize is certainly hungry, and would not be able to pay a high fine." With a highly pragmatic sense of what is appropriate she points out that the cost of keeping someone in prison for such a long period of time "far outweighs the cost of the chicken or the bag of maize." In her view alternatives to imprisonment must be found and implemented, and criminal laws "must be amended so as not to give lower courts too much room to manoeuvre in the sentencing of offenders."

Being someone who does not merely see a problem and analyse the background to the problem, Rahila can also discern potential solutions. The criminal justice system in Nigeria she feels is in need of an approach which concentrates on rehabilitation. Perhaps the time has therefore come to introduce community-based sentences into the criminal justice system as an alternative to imprisonment. "This may be the solution to the problems of prison congestion in this country that have so far defied all solutions."

Under her leadership as the Chief Judge of Kaduna State, all the High Court Judges in the State now have their individual court rooms equipped with recording machines. Each one of them also has a laptop. This will certainly make the dispensation of justice a lot faster. The judiciary in Kaduna State also has an ultra modern Conference Hall with a full Multimedia Projector, a Screen and a Computer Workstation.

Outside interests

Perhaps the reason that Rahila is held in such high regard by so many of the legal profession and has been honoured with the award of Officer of the Order of the Federal Republic (OFR), is that she is motivated by so much more than blind adherence to the letter of the Law. While recognising that the rule of Law is essential in any civilised society, she also considers that such a society will make most progress if it recognises the talents of its women.

Consequently Rahila is very proud of the progress that Nigeria has made in implementing the Beijing Platform for Action as the result of the 1995 UN World Conference on Women. Many Nigerian women have now been able to penetrate the metaphorical "glass ceiling," which had previously prevented them from taking their true position in Nigerian society. This has been as the result of Federal and State action and the Platform for Action itself which has been widely circulated in Nigeria after being translated into local languages. She is clearly very proud that "concrete steps have been taken to integrate women into development programmes at the local levels, so that even women at the grass-roots level are being brought into the limelight at all levels of government, whether local, State or Federal."

It is also important in her view that society learns how to deal with and to combat the scourge of AIDS, of growing concern to the rest of the world, but so particularly serious for Africa. The Federal Ministry of Health has projected that if nothing is done to curb the HIV/AIDS pandemic before 2015, there would be a faster rise in AIDS related deaths than in deaths caused by either malaria or measles. She was therefore part of an International Group at the Commonwealth Judicial Education Institute (CJEI) that looked at the topic "HIV Law and Justice to Women" with the view of designing a toolkit for training judicial officers and staff on contributing their quota towards combating the scourge. She is of the view that judicial officers have to be more proactive in interpreting laws that are prejudicial to women and their rights

Rahila is one of the founding members and first treasurer of the National Association of Women Judges (NAWJ) inaugurated in Lagos in 1991 and also one of the founding members of the International Association of Women Judges (IAWJ) inaugurated in San Diego, California, U.S.A in 1992. She is a member of the National Association for Court Management, U.S.A and fellow of the Commonwealth Judicial Education Institute (CJEI), Halifax, Canada.

She was married and has two children.

Ameze Guobadia

Ameze Guobadia was appointed Director General of the Nigerian Institute of Advanced Legal Studies in 2003.

Courteous and thoughtful, Ameze Guobadia dislikes publicity, speaks in public only if it is to advance the cause of legal education and of NIALS in particular and only when it is absolutely necessary. She is focused, hard working and overwhelmingly concerned about improving the standards of legal education and its provision in Nigeria.

Early days

Ameze was born in Ibadan but because her father, who came from the ancient Bini Kingdom was subsequently transferred to Lagos, she received her primary school education at Our Lady of the Apostles Private School in Yaba and her secondary school education at Queen's College Yaba, Lagos. However, when her father was then transferred to Benin she spent her final year at primary school in her ancestral home. This seemed to him a unique opportunity to familiarise his young family with their roots, and for Ameze this short spell of time in Benin was "pleasant and a bit of an adventure." Being an adaptable child, she did not find it difficult to settle into life in this new environment before returning to Lagos.

Ameze points out that "there was no fancy lawyer in the family that inspired in me a burning desire to become one myself, but it was always drummed into me from an early age that in making any career choice I should be looking for a profession." She did not excel in science subjects and with a definite penchant for English and English Literature and the Arts generally, she felt that the most logical thing to do was to read Law. "Indeed if it had not been impressed upon me from such an early age that I had to follow a course of study leading to a profession, perhaps I would have studied English Literature because that was my first love and it has remained an enduring interest." Indeed, she admits that if she were ever to return to study, she would most likely study English Literature. "I still have an abiding love for English Literature. There is nothing quite like it. I still enjoy Chaucer, Shakespeare and simple prose and poetry, indeed anything in the written form. I do not see it as an alternative to what I have done, because I have found contentment in my academic life in research in Law, but it is an additional interest that I would pursue given the opportunity."

Making the choice

Like many other lawyers before her and since, she admits that "of course I watched movies with legal themes such as the court room drama involving the fictional character *Perry Mason*," and although she had found them interesting, they in themselves would certainly not have been sufficient to direct her subsequent choice of career. The decision to study

Law was really influenced by a combination of factors, and she is at pains to point out that her parents gave her complete autonomy in making her career choice and did not try to impose any choice one way or the other.

In his own very quiet way, Ameze's father has been her biggest champion and has always been very supportive of her career decision. "He is not demonstrative about it but he was always there to back me all the way. I never obtained a scholarship, and he paid my fees and continued to support me."

Becoming an academic

The Law is a very wide country and for each lawyer there is some motivating factor that suggests the choice of one state over another. In Ameze's case it was probably an intense love of learning that influenced her towards academic life as opposed to private practice or being in house counsel. Ameze had enjoyed her period of study as an undergraduate at the University of Lagos, had revelled in the intellectual stimulation and friendliness of campus life and felt that she would benefit from more of the same. It was therefore an easy choice to continue with a further period of more advanced legal study at University College, London, to obtain her Master's Degree. Although she did in fact spend a brief period in private practice in Benin after obtaining her professional qualification at the Nigerian Law School, Providence intervened and she was invited to join the teaching staff in the newly created Law Faculty of the University of Benin by Mr. R.A. Williams, then Registrar of the University. She was interviewed by Professor I.E. Sagay, the first Dean of Law at the University and he encouraged her to come on board. She accepted the invitation and thus made the leap into academia where she has been ever since.

There were certainly challenges inherent in her new position. Ameze was not much older than her students and some were in fact older than she was, so that the first challenge was about discovering how to exert the authority required to be an effective lecturer. "But I was fortunate to have Professor Sagay as my Dean as he was a solid academic and very supportive of all his staff." It was also a time when "Universities were not in decline." Students came into the tertiary education system with relatively good basic education and were able and willing to learn. Tutorials were still a feature of student study life and Ameze looked forward to tutorials. "I gave them things to read, which they did read, and then they would come to class and challenge me." For someone so committed to teaching and education this was a very exciting environment in which to work. "For many years I taught Company Law as well as Constitutional Law. I had just come back from the Masters programme and was full of fresh ideas. Reforms were taking place in the wider world and we at home were also looking at these issues, so I was very much in touch and comfortable with what I was teaching. I subscribed to the articles and journals and would give the students topics ahead of the tutorials to prepare. They prepared well and would come to class and give me a run for my money. I enjoyed that thoroughly. It was inspiring."

Unfortunately as the years went by the decline in standards in the university environment "became very clear." Teachers could no longer count on having students who were genuinely interested. "They were coming in with diverse educational backgrounds and studying was certainly not the priority for many of them. Some had no real interest in actually learning and knowing the Law. For some of them, if it had been possible to get a certificate and get out in two weeks that would have been enough." In line with the general economic decline in society the universities were no longer being funded properly and consequently the enabling environment for academic work was slowly eroded. Inevitably "class sizes got larger and larger. One of the challenges we are facing right now is how to manage ordered growth."

Then and now

When Ameze was an undergraduate those students who were studying Law in Nigeria were well supported both by staff and facilities. The libraries were well stocked and "we had a full complement of inspiring senior level staff. These were people who had themselves been taught by the authors of the text books we were using. They had received the best in their own time and so it was very easy for them to impart the best to us. The classes were not large and so we all knew each other by name and developed very friendly relationships." Students studied together and a substantial part of the teaching time was set aside for compulsory tutorials. "Because of this there was a lot of brainstorming and we enjoyed all these different facets of student life. It was fun and we had no choice but to use our minds"

This, she comments sadly, is very different from the current situation in most universities. "The classes are choked, and a system of course credits has been introduced in a system that cannot provide teaching for each course all year round as is done elsewhere. This means that students are over tested in terms of the number of times they undertake exams, but I am not too sure about the depth of their knowledge because I do not know how much knowledge they could have acquired in the short time left between sitting all those exams. And staff are over worked because they are constantly marking exam papers." She feels that lecturers are so burdened with administrative tasks that they are left with no time to research and prepare their lectures properly. "I really do not believe that students studying Law today in the current higher education setting are getting the same added value that students were privileged to receive in my time as an undergraduate."

Conditions at the Nigerian Law School were also different for Ameze and her peers. They were "idyllic. We benefited from smaller classes and formed small working groups to study after classes. It was a good time to study as the economy was much better and society was undoubtedly safer. Student groups would study together and relax together at the nearby snack bars. We looked forward to each day and many of us have kept those ties over the years." Thus, lasting friendships were formed from their positive shared educational experience. Now there is a backlog of students waiting for an opportunity to take the professional exams and classes are much larger, which she believes cannot produce the same educational experience.

Women lawyers

Ameze does not take a gender approach but a human approach to women's place in society. She believes that all human beings have certain skills and that the important thing is to use the skills that you have. "You could be a good cook or a good mason. It has nothing to do with gender. However, in the context of our society where a woman is still expected to manage the home, Law is a good option because it is so versatile and you can combine it with your family obligations." It also has the added advantage that it is adaptable to most mainstream career paths, and can be helpful for those pursuing a career in administration or in the Civil Service, as well as traditional private practice among others. "It is also uniquely advantageous if you are by nature a champion of causes because it equips you for this role. Similarly, if your desire is to be a politician, there is no training better than legal training, as it gives you the basic skills needed to succeed in this area. For women who may not wish to work but still want to use their brains, it is also an intellectually stimulating option."

Ameze now has many responsibilities which would not be associated in the public's mind as belonging to the realm of the lawyer, and her working days as Director General of the NIALS are therefore very unpredictable, especially as at present she shuttles between Abuja and Lagos in the course of her work. Although technically her appointment as Director General is a political one, she regards herself also as an academic who is "saddled with administrative tasks because of my position." This does not mean that she does not take these duties any the less seriously than academic research, because she knows that good administrative oversight is necessary to ensure that NIALS functions effectively and efficiently. Towards her aim of providing "a serene environment for work and learning," she spends a great deal of time putting proper budgeting and planning systems in place. "I am not unmindful of the need to be there to take care of these issues. If there is a leak in the roof of the building, it gets to my table. If I was simply a researcher, I could get on with academic work and my day would be very different."

There is an implicit sense that at this point in her life restricting her activities only to the academic would not be altogether satisfying for someone who sees her legal training and experience as tools which could be used to make a difference in other people's lives, and who feels a strong impulse of responsibility to give the best educational opportunity that she can to Nigeria's legal professionals. As all this work could potentially take a toll on her physical wellbeing, she tries to place some health-giving structure into every day – and this is the only predictable part of her working life.

She attempts to start each day with Prayers and the Scriptures, some exercise, a walk in the early hours of the morning or some light exercise at home, and makes an effort to have breakfast as she is in the habit of working through the day without a break for lunch. "I get in and get started and by the time I look up again the day is long gone. The day just goes despite all my efforts. There are times when I am determined not to work too late, but then I look up and I realise that the day is gone" As a practising Catholic she finds strength in visiting "the blessed sacrament" and will routinely stop by the church at some point daily and sit quietly for a while. "I draw my strength from that. I also try to make a habit of daily Mass."

At the end of the day, on those days when there is an end to the working day, Ameze unwinds with a book. "I read. I am probably what can be described as an avid reader. Novels, books on philosophy, law books, magazines - comics when I find them -anything in fact. I also listen to music as I find music very relaxing. Way back I tried a bit of golf but have not kept it up. I am introspective and like to spend quiet time alone. I also like going to the theatre and cooking and entertaining friends at home in small groups. It is very relaxing to enjoy a good glass of wine with friends over dinner."

On success

Ameze says that she read some words once in a goodwill card which sum up her attitude to life. "They were 'May you always strive and may you never arrive.' In other words the sky should be your limit." With that in mind, she would like to believe that any career high point is still ahead. She acknowledges that becoming a full Professor of Law is regarded as being the apex of professional achievement in academia, but that is certainly not something that such a complex person would rest on as being sufficient in itself, mainly because it would lend an air of finality to an already glittering career, which for Ameze is definitely not over.

Asked to speak about success therefore and what it might mean to her, she chooses to comment on something which is almost intangible, often unacknowledged and very personal. "As someone once said, there is a moment of fulfilment for every artist and that comes at the culmination of art and audience. At different points I have had a feeling of fulfilment, sometimes at conferences when I have been asked to address an audience and I feel I have caught their attention and sold an idea to them. Their response can be very fulfilling. I experienced this at the Commonwealth Law Conference in Malaysia. I have also experienced it when I have come across former students who introduce themselves with a lot of goodwill pointing out that – oh you taught me such and such." She adds quietly that since becoming Director General some of the projects undertaken by NIALS have also produced similar satisfaction when they are presented to the general public and appreciated. These are activities such as the first Fellows Lecture which has been received with critical acclaim from the profession and the revival of the lecture series in honour of the late Taslim Elias, the first Nigerian to be appointed Attorney General and Minister of Justice of the Federation.

She is also satisfied with the increasing subscriptions for the Institute's programmes, and for the Legal Writing Skills courses instituted for practitioners and academics. There are so many other things of which she and NIALS are justly proud - the newly introduced course on International Criminal Justice and its Administration, the efforts put into developing the NIALS Library collections as a resource for academics and practitioners and also the NIALS Scholars Scheme which was set up to provide short periods of supervised research training for young lecturers. This is all part of her effort to redress the difficulties faced by academics in Nigeria. These really come down to a dearth of funds which inhibit their access to research material and their ability to undertake continuous professional development. If you are an academic, "it is important to attend conferences and to interact with your peers as every opportunity utilised in this way helps to show you just what your limitations are and how you might try to do better."

Being a lawyer

The opportunity to be a lawyer in Ameze's view is a call to shoulder responsibility. Legal training of itself does two things. At the moment you are enrolled as a lawyer, you are first acknowledged as having acquired some very sophisticated tools to work with, and second you enter a certain echelon of society. "If you are going to take these privileges then you must also take the responsibility that goes with them. That means that if you are teaching Law, you must do what is right and prepare your lectures properly. You must be prepared to attend all the lectures for which you are time-tabled and be accountable."

It is necessary therefore before embarking on a career in the Law to recognise that it will require study both before and after qualification. "Mathematics, at least to O Level Pass level, should be a compulsory requirement for potential lawyers, because basic Mathematics is as essential as basic English. Indeed, it should be more than basic English – a good command of the language is essential." She also suggests that a study of Literature and Literary Appreciation would be more than useful as familiarity with these Arts subjects could considerably enhance an individual's skill as a lawyer. "I remind students that a Law degree is the beginning of their careers and not the end of it. It is simply a means to an end and their careers then depend on what they themselves make of them." The key lesson to take away from Ameze's own career in the Law is "commitment. Pace yourself, set your goals and do not let anything derail you. You do not have to be the most brilliant individual, if you can be the one who is identified as the hard worker, because it is in reality hard work and commitment and the grace of God that will get you to your goal."

Priscilla Kuye

Priscilla Kuye is the Head of Priscilla O Kuye & Co. She was also the first woman to become President of the Nigerian Bar Association and the first woman to become President of the Nigerian American Chamber of Commerce.

Early years

Although from Ogun State, Priscilla was born in Lagos, but in common with many Nigerians did not spend her childhood in one place. She attended primary school in Ibadan and received part of her secondary school education at St. Ann's Lagos, where she passed the entrance examination for St. Anne's School in Ibadan. "But because I'm a Catholic, the Reverend Sisters asked my parents not to send me there, saying that I should have a Catholic education. So, I went to St Teresa's College in Ibadan from Forms Three to Five." Priscilla then completed her academic education in London and remained to study Law, where she became a member of Gray's Inn.

On choosing Law as a profession

Both Priscilla's parents had attended Yaba College in Lagos, which in their day provided the equivalent of a university education. "Not many people at that time had the opportunity to study to that level and certainly not many women." The inspiration behind Priscilla's desire to study Law was her mother, a trained teacher, who had always had this one unfulfilled ambition. "She kept saying that she would return to school to study Law; even when she was very old, she was insisting 'I must read Law.'" Priscilla is at pains to point out that this was not a case of a parent foisting her thwarted ambitions on a child; rather Priscilla's mother created a curiosity about the possibilities of following a particular field of study, "so because my mother kept insisting she was going to read Law, I started wondering what it was in Law that made my mother want to study it, when she was a very good teacher, a headmistress and was well respected in our society. And she was also someone who found time to be a woman activist and a politician."

Briefly Priscilla considered medicine as a career because she wanted to do something that would be of direct help to people, but that ambition foundered on her scientific ability, or rather lack of it. "I guess it wasn't my line, because I got stuck with my Chemistry. I wasn't very brilliant at that, although in Arts subjects, I was good. So I said, I too will read Law since my mother was so keen. And that was how I decided to read Law."

Despite that decision, Priscilla still went on to train as a State Registered Nurse (SRN) at St Bartholomew's Hospital, not far from St Paul's Cathedral in London. "I just wanted to look after people. I went there to qualify, but I never really practised what I had learned." Immediately afterwards Priscilla enrolled at Gray's Inn, which coincidentally was only a short walk away from the hospital where she had done her training, and began her LLB degree in London. Priscilla explains that English legal training is very different from legal training in Nigeria. By studying at Gray's Inn Priscilla became a barrister, whose work is very much Court based, rather than a solicitor, whose activities are much more office based. In Nigeria these two aspects of legal work are combined, but in England they are separate. After graduation in August 1966 Priscilla came home to attend Law School, was enrolled at the Supreme Court and started practising straight away. "I began with senior lawyer John Edwin Burke of Burke & Co in 1970 and then I started my own practice. And since then, I've been in practice."

Private practice

"When I started at first, I had to learn the ropes by working with a senior who had a very good Commercial Law practice. We registered trademarks, incorporated companies, did joint venture agreements and many other things associated with commercial practice, so I was learning. It was very hard work as we had to be in the chambers by 8 am and didn't close until about 6 pm sometimes."

Priscilla has thought carefully about how women may succeed in "having it all," the catchphrase current at the time when she set up in practice. "It is certainly possible to work from home once you have built up your own reputation as a good lawyer. Then people will come to you. But when you're just starting, go to a good chambers, find a good senior and learn the ropes and then when you have done all that, you can be on your own." But she also points out that even with a reputation for excellent work, "it's good to have other lawyers to assist you because the work is very strenuous. I have cases all over the place, in Abuja, in Kaduna and in Ibadan and sometimes it is impossible to do it all, so I send my junior lawyers. However, when it comes to the hearing, I like to handle the cases myself. Like I said, hard work never killed anybody."

Priscilla states firmly that setting up as a sole practitioner is not an easy option. She could not afford to make mistakes. "What I believe is that you must prepare every case that you are given very, very thoroughly. Anything that your client gives you, do it to the best of your ability. When I'm preparing a case, I do my research and write my questions down so that when I get to Court, I don't have to fumble. You have to devote time to getting and briefing your witnesses, getting them to speak the truth about the matter or what happened. All of that is important. Then gradually things will progress, and when you satisfy one client, that client will bring you more. That was how my own chambers started to grow. Now I have many lawyers in the Chambers with a lot of support staff, and I thank God for that.

She is proud that, "there is nothing we cannot handle in our chambers." This is achieved by permitting her lawyers to focus on their own specialist areas and skills. They are not all advocates. Although some are certainly interested in advocacy, others concentrate more on chamber work such as the drafting of documents, negotiating joint ventures and registering companies, trademarks and patents. "I also have lawyers interested in Petroleum Law, Property Law, and arbitration. It's a wide range as you can see."

Women in the Law

From those early days when Priscilla began in practice, there has been much alteration in the daily life of women in Nigeria, and not just in terms of how professional women are treated. However, it has been at the professional level that perhaps the changes in the perceived position of women in society have been most obvious. As Priscilla points out, "There were certainly men then who felt that women should be in the kitchen, making babies and cooking. But one thing I respect men for, is that once they know you know your onions and that you work hard, they respect you for it. I used to tell them that there was no reason I could not be a professional and be a good advocate just like them, and they respect you for that." Even in the Seventies there were very few women in private practice; the preferred career pattern for women was to go to the Ministry of Justice and then possibly to go to work for a company.

"Actually, being in private practice is hard work. Especially when preparing your cases, as in order to present just one case, you might have to read more than twenty or twenty-five authorities as part of the preparation." Priscilla's point is simply that for many women the sheer unpredictability and sudden demands of private practice make it impossible to produce any sort of settled professional life that could be combined with family life. She certainly does not think that women are incapable of the hard work required.

Priscilla is of the opinion that, "one of the deterrents to women entering private practice is simply combining long work hours with family life. This can even now be very difficult for some young women because their husbands don't want them to work. I have friends where the husbands recognise that their wives are graduates, but still say, "No I don't want you to work. Sit at home." And I think that is very bad, it is a great waste." A waste it may be, but Priscilla does not play down the sheer physical exertion required by those who undertake her chosen profession.

The Law and family life

"It is strenuous, it is very strenuous." She also emphasises that an ability to plan and organise your time well is essential because of the conflicting demands that will be made if a woman lawyer has a husband and children. "You may have to give up some things because of your children and your family. You should put your family first, that is very important. I believe that sometimes if women want to have babies they should choose a profession where they can work from their home. This is especially true now when it is difficult to get good nannies. Maybe that's why women prefer going to the Ministries where they can work from 8 am to 3 pm, which just isn't possible if you're in practice. Sometimes I'm in chambers until about 7pm or later."

"I have a very understanding and supportive husband, who doesn't mind when I'm working very hard in the Chambers, because he believes every human being should develop his or her potential. I know some men don't want their wives to be heard, but my husband encourages me. But, and this is very important, I never let the home suffer." Priscilla's husband, a lawyer and an economist, who worked in the Civil Service while the children were growing up, and whose working day finished earlier than hers, was happy to operate in partnership with her when it came to looking after the children. The children were always collected from school by a trustworthy driver. If possible Priscilla would pick them up with the driver, but whether she was there or not, her husband would always be at home in time to ensure a parental presence when they arrived. "I have had to organise my time and learn to prioritise. When there are parties, I may not go, because it is important to spend time at home with the children or with my family. You have to prioritise what is important to you at any given time when you are building up your career, but you should never let your home suffer."

Gender discrimination?

Priscilla does not consider that she has been the victim of any overt gender discrimination, and by the way that she considers this concept she clearly does not feel that it is an endemic problem in the legal profession in Nigeria. Clients in her view will not be biased against being assisted by a woman lawyer if she can obtain the results that they want. "Clients come to you because they trust you. I work for many companies, and I know that clients will come to you if they know that you are skilled and that you know your profession."

She is however, somewhat amused by her experience with the Nigerian Bar Association, of which she became the first female President in 1991. In Priscilla's view a lawyer should join the NBA in order to serve other lawyers and the cause of justice in the country, not merely to acquire power or an extra line on a CV, so that when she became a member of the Lagos Bar, she attended the meetings regularly. This got her noticed and led to an invitation to become a member of the Lagos Branch Executive. As she became more involved with the work of the Lagos Branch she noticed that the male members were standing for various senior offices within the NBA, "and I said that I too would like to stand for these offices. When they realised that I was serious, they sent me as a representative to the National Body where I became a member of the National Executive on which very few women have sat."

At that point Priscilla formed the ambition to become the first woman President of the NBA, and served as Financial Secretary, then as Third, Second and First Vice President. "The interesting thing was that men didn't have to climb this career progression ladder, but it was decided that if a woman was going to be the National President of the NBA, she must do this," presumably to prove her worth and to attest to her determination. The NBA had been in existence for about a hundred years before it succeeded in electing its first ever female President, but unfortunately, as a result of the intervention of President Babangida's government which wanted to dictate the demographic origins of NBA

Presidents, her tenure was cut short. However, "I pray many more women will make it. That was the only bit of discrimination I can remember being directed towards me. But what amuses me was that although men respect you for what you are, there is often still a little bit of them that remains chauvinistic."

Achievements

Priscilla's CV runs over several pages of success in her chosen profession, election to high office in various organisations, memberships of organisations set up to help others, public service assignments and honours, but she has a highly pragmatic attitude to success. "I've handled many cases. You win some, you lose some. A lawyer cannot expect to be winning cases all the time, but there are some which if you win, give you particular satisfaction."

In one land case a woman from Edo State with four children lost her husband and his relatives wanted to take over the husband's company, which was a very substantial enterprise. "I handled the case for her and won it in the High Court. Then the husband's relatives who were opposing her and who wanted a share in the company decided to go to the Court of Appeal. I won the case there too. She got her husband's company back, so that she could maintain her children. The relatives said that they were going to go to the Supreme Court, but they didn't." There is a distinct impression that if they had chosen to take that final step, Priscilla would have been ready for them.

Success however can come in many guises, not all of them personally public, and Priscilla has particular praise for those women's organisations like Zonta, to which she belongs, which work to raise the status of women by taking steps to empower them. It gives her pleasure to say that Zonta

members have given time to run a basic literacy course for
market women so that they would be able to read and write.

The frustrations of private practice

Long hours and peremptory client demands are not the
only difficulties facing lawyers in private practice. The
adjournment of cases in court after substantial preparation
can be excessively frustrating. "But now, with the new High
Court Procedure Rules in Lagos, I think that the trials are
faster. When you file a case now, you have to file all your
exhibits, sort out the witnesses and then hold a pre-trial
conference to demonstrate whether you really have a serious
case. There are also Hearings for Directions like they have in
England and lawyers are fined if they are supposed to file
something and it is not done at a particular time. Certain
areas in the new High Court Procedure Rules may still require
amendment and a seminar was organised recently to
consider potential areas for amendment."

What the Law requires

It is essential that both men and women realise that they
need to have great integrity when they come into the
profession. Working hard has a dual purpose. First, a lawyer
must work hard to promote the client's interest and second
"must work hard to make a good living." This may seem a
strange injunction from a woman who has been
emphasising service to the community, but Priscilla believes
that lawyers have a responsibility to society to earn enough
money so that they will not be tempted to steal their clients'
money. Clients are entitled to believe that when they give
lawyers large amounts of money to pay into their client
accounts, those lawyers are not going to appropriate the
money for some other selfish purpose entirely.

Being able to make a good living also enables lawyers to give something back to the community. "I am able to do pro bono cases too for people who are poor, because there are some poor clients who cannot afford lawyers and I think lawyers should help them when they can."

The temptations are there for those lawyers who are less competent. And Priscilla has a real concern for the future of the legal profession in her native country. "At the moment I think lawyers are doing their best but there is a problem in that standards have fallen because some of the universities are not able to provide the education that they were able to in the past." This has been taken so seriously that recently in Abuja a seminar was held to consider what can be done about the falling standards of education in certain Nigerian universities. "In the past we had dedicated people as lecturers, but now they are not able to give their full attention to the students. I don't know whether this is because of the economy, but it certainly is not like it was in the old days when the teachers were one hundred percent dedicated. It is very difficult for lecturers when they don't get their salaries in time; instead of devoting all their attention to their students they are forced to spend their time selling this and that to make ends meet. I hope it improves."

This means that older lawyers in practice have an additional responsibility to the future of Law in Nigeria. "In the case of some young lawyers, you have to supervise everything that they do. When they write letters, you must check those letters. Maybe it's because they are fresh from College, and because practice is so very different from academic study. Unfortunately I notice that the standards of graduates who come from Nigeria could certainly be better."

None of this is irretrievable. However, it does mean that an even greater onus is placed on young lawyers to be alert and to make the best of their abilities. "Young lawyers should make up their minds to work hard, to be honest, to be prepared to acquire knowledge and to continue their education. We must be prepared to embrace new technology and to keep updating our knowledge with the help of computers and the internet."

In summary

"On reflection, I think that for me Law is the best profession. I'm very happy that I'm a lawyer because it is such a versatile profession. Lawyers have the opportunity to help a great many people. You can use your legal skills to be a business man or woman or a politician. When you know the Law, nobody can cheat you unless you want to be cheated, and as a lawyer and a politician you can contribute to the development of the nation. The Law is an excellent profession, which I have not regretted joining. I think God knew what He was doing when he made me a lawyer."

Ayo Obe

Ayo Obe was the second female President of the Civil Liberties Organisation, and chaired the Transition Monitoring Group from 1999 to 2001. She is currently in private practice in Lagos and is also a member of the Nigeria Police Service Commission and of the CLEEN (Centre for Law Enforcement Education Nigeria) Foundation.

Ayo Obe is articulate, assertive and opinionated, attributes which in a tradition-bound society like Nigeria are unusual in a woman. She certainly does not conform to any ideal of a Nigerian woman as being demure and self-effacing. Ayo is a woman who likes to deviate from the norm, a rule breaker who has allowed neither her gender nor society's expectations of women's behaviour to affect her objectives in life.

Background details

Ayo's childhood was in many ways predetermined and uneventful, but her tendency to argue and to question the status quo began to surface when she was studying for her Masters Degree in the United Kingdom. "I was born in the United Kingdom, where I attended Highbury Hill High School, and did everything at the usual ages. I went to secondary school at the age of eleven, finished at eighteen with my A Levels, then went on to do my first degree at

Cardiff University and the second one, on the New International Economic Order, at the University of Wales."

Professor Brown, an acknowledged expert on International Law, was her tutor on this course. It did not take Ayo long to decide that his definition of "International" Law was very limited and was applied to situations only if Britain, France or the United States were involved in some way. "So I would ask him how did Law become international just because the United Kingdom had a hand in it." At that time, OPEC (Organisation of Petroleum Exporting Countries) was beginning to flex its muscles, and as a consequence of the Arab-Israeli War in the Middle East in 1973 had doubled and tripled the price of oil per barrel. "Suddenly there was talk about a new international economic order where developing countries who were up to that point just selling raw materials at prices offered by others, were going to be able to dictate the prices of those raw materials." This for Ayo was where the word "international" should be truly applied, when it referred to a multitude of nation states not just to an Old World coterie.

Coming home

Returning to Nigeria in the mid Seventies and attending the Nigerian Law School made Ayo realise that her secondary school experience had been very different from that of the other female students. Her father had been one of the first students at the Nigerian Law School in the early Sixties. He had sufficient influence to suggest that the Law School Hostel at Igbosere Road in Lagos, which had become too small for the male students, was just the right size for the new intake of female students, which included his daughter.

"Although I went to boarding school, I had not had the type of communal life that most Nigerian girls had had in secondary school or university." This showed in various ways, some social and some educational. Those students who had "foreign" degrees were required to take an additional course lasting a term which was usually held in the afternoon for about an hour or so. And perhaps influenced by her mother's profession as a sociologist Ayo used to stand on her balcony and "watch the world go by. I soon discovered that I was getting a rash on my forearms, which was a clear indication that I was probably spending too much time on the balcony!" (There is very little chance of being exposed to too much sun in Wales.) While the other girls were dressed in Yves Saint Laurent with their hair coiffured and permed, Ayo "had this low cut hair style" and spoke with a strong English accent so that "whereas other people felt free about talking, I tried to keep my mouth shut," a feat which it is very hard to imagine now.

Why Law?

Ayo's mother was a sociologist and her father was a lawyer. As her sister studied sociology there can be a supposition that Ayo studied Law just to maintain the family symmetry. "But actually to me a Law degree was a kind of good entrée into lots of different fields. After a Law Degree you could go into business or whatever else you wanted to do." Ayo regarded her time studying Law as a "kind of general education" which would complete the studying part of her life.

Both parents assumed that Ayo would have a career. Her mother, who came from Ijebuland, was a Controller in LSDPC (Lagos State Development and Property Corporation) when she retired, so it was not a strange concept in Ayo's family that women should work or be educated. Ayo remarks with some pride that her mother had received a sound education in exactly the same way as her brothers and sisters.

While at university in the United Kingdom and as befits someone who has been so active in standing up for the rights of those she has described as "the voiceless" she considered for a while operating in a more international sphere. "I used to think that I would like to work for something like the United Nations, but in the end, I realised the extent to which the UN was in the pocket of the US. And I thought that if I worked there, I would be worrying about whether my salary would be dependent on the whims of the US. So I decided not to look for a UN job."

After Law School Ayo worked out her compulsory NYSC year in Kano. As young lawyers both she and her colleagues knew that they would be sent either to work in the Ministry of Justice on Legal Aid matters or to assist in a Government office. In fact "we started off with the Legal Aid Scheme but as they couldn't provide us with accommodation the Ministry of Justice took us over. We oscillated between the two of them. I can't remember going to Court or doing anything connected with Court." Again this is an important omission for someone who has spent her professional life in very difficult advocacy situations.

The independent young lawyer

After NYSC, Ayo joined her father's practice in his home city of Ibadan. This was where "I first learned how to draft a motion and how to address a Court. It really hadn't sunk in while I was at Law School." But Ayo found working for her father extremely difficult. "You can't be your own person when you are working for your father. I admire my colleagues who work for their dads, because parents can be real tyrants." Fortunately, one of her friends asked Chief G.O.K Ajayi whether he could employ her. Although his Chambers were full at that time, he later remembered Ayo when he had a vacancy. "So I went to Lagos which infuriated my father," because in his view Ayo had gone "around looking for a job without telling him. It didn't really occur to me to inform him about it. Having been brought up in England, I had learned to be independent, and at university, although I had a grant, it was quite small so during my first year in university, I had to do a part-time job to earn money."

Because Ayo had learned typing at school she went to a secretarial agency "where I was asked if I could type and I said yes." That was how Ayo became a copy typist in the days before word processing. "You had carbon papers and if you made mistakes, you had to erase everything and start all over again." Instead of spending her time on leisure pursuits Ayo carried on working as a copy typist during her vacations in order to pay her way.

She does not consider that having to contribute to her educational costs was any sort of disadvantage, because it helped her to develop a "certain degree of independence, the ability to look after yourself. It didn't occur to me to go to my dad and say Daddy, I need a job can you help me?" But sometimes even Ayo has needed a little push to get her going. While at Chief Ajayi's Chambers she needed the encouragement of her boyfriend to ask for an increase in salary on the grounds that she had a Masters Degree and should therefore earn at least 400 naira a month more than those of her classmates who didn't have the same qualifications.

Chief Ajayi must have been truly astonished, because before Ayo came to work with him, he held the biased belief that "women can't work and can't stand the pace. That was his prejudice." The only woman who had worked there before Ayo was Mary Bassey who left to follow another path and "is now one of the most eminent members of the

Nigerian Bar." But by the time Ayo left eleven years later, Chief Ajayi admitted that "he needed another woman like me. What this shows is that gender is not relevant when it comes to work. The important thing is just to do anything worth doing as well as you can."

Working for Ajayi

In September 1979 Ayo began working for Chief Ajayi. At his chambers there was very little "solicitor work" in the way of conveyancing, dealing with wills and probate and contract drafting. The practice was almost entirely Litigation based, so that his lawyers were constantly in Court. When Ayo went to Court for the first time, "clamping the wig and gown on and having to say something," the other lawyers were very supportive and whispered instructions about what to say if she could not understand or hear the judge. "The next day, we were in the middle of a very important case and my name was on the list of twenty three lawyers who appeared for Chief Obafemi Awolowo."

Chief Ajayi was a very precise man. "We started work at 7.30 in the morning and closed at 4.45 in the afternoon. You hardly had any time to breathe. Ajayi was time conscious, and did not believe in "African time." If people came late, he used to send them away, even if they were his own lawyers." However, Ayo remembers with approval that "he was always very supportive and understood that those who don't make mistakes, never learn." He proved an excellent mentor to her.

Ayo had decided to "try this wig and gown stuff" while she could afford to make those mistakes. Despite the perceived drawbacks of practising Litigation in Nigeria Ayo finds the whole experience stimulating. She lists the difficulties of court practice in Nigeria as having proceedings taken down in long hand, there being no jury on a day-to- day basis and the sporadic nature of the process, where "you do something for a couple of hours and then you resume about three months later." This she recognises can "put the client in a tight situation."

The political dimension

Chief Ajayi was lawyer to Chief Awolowo, and so his chambers became involved in the big constitutional cases between the UPN (Unity Party of Nigeria) and the NPN (National Party of Nigeria) which gave Ayo exposure to "all kinds of interesting things. By the time we got to the 1983 elections, we had two major sets of cases, one, in which I was not personally involved, concerned the governorship of Ondo State. The other was in Jos where we were doing cases in Plateau State concerning irregularities in the election process". The NPN had by chicanery managed to have a declaration made that they had been victorious in many of the elections and had won many seats in the State House of Assembly. This was of particular concern to the Governor of Plateau State because he did not want to work with an NPN-dominated House.

In spite of all the travelling involved and often having to stay up all night, Ayo found the work fascinating and exciting. "The first time I was permitted to file a case, the Governor, Chief Solomon Lar, the founder of the PDP (People's Democratic Party), asked who was this small girl that Chief Ajayi had sent, and demanded to know why he couldn't come himself. Perhaps he was expecting someone big, although by then as I was twenty-eight, I could hardly be described as a "small" girl."

Whatever her size, her legal skills were clearly appreciated by Chief Ajayi for, after two years, when she was the most senior person working for him, he made her his Head of Chambers.

She continued in this position until her daughter, Funmilola, was born. "Then I needed to have more control over my time-table than working in the Chambers would provide."

This did not mean that she gave up work or responsibility. In 1991 Supo Shonibare, a lawyer who had worked with Chief Ajayi, set up his own practice and was looking for a partner. Ayo considered the possibilities carefully. "I didn't feel I could go out and get business myself. I couldn't see myself going around and asking people to give me work. So I said that if he would get the jobs, I would be the tiller of the soil so to speak." They set up in practice as Ogunsola Shonibare.

Discrimination in court?

Perhaps because, although Nigerian, she was not brought up in Nigeria, Ayo occupies an interesting middle ground of understanding what it is to be a Nigerian woman, but being also able to observe more clearly what are the benefits and drawbacks of being one. Ayo has campaigned on behalf of the rights of many of her countrywomen, but she is very careful not to say that she speaks for all Nigerian women "I can only say that I feel as myself and not generically for all women," as she is aware that she does not come across as the archetypal Nigerian woman. On one occasion she was asked why she was "talking as a man." What the questioner really meant was not that she had a big voice, but that she was not talking with due deference. But she says with a resigned smile, "It's how I am. Here Yoruba girls are taught to worry about finding husbands and that they will not marry if they behave in a certain way. So their behaviour becomes a big issue, whereas to me it simply never was."

She is also aware that being a woman advocate in Court can cause difficulties in certain situations. "In one case I was examining a man wearing the ankara of Government

College, Ibadan, from the same set as my father. I had to ask him about the internal injuries a woman was supposed to have sustained in the course of adultery. It was quite difficult. I'm not a simperer. Another woman would have burst into tears but I didn't think it would work for me." Ever the pragmatist, she simply assessed the situation, realised that her potential embarrassment at having to examine a man of her father's generation on details of female biology was simply irrelevant to the case at hand, and got on with it. Ayo narrates this incident to indicate the sort of difficulties which arise when women apparently act against cultural norms, but she also says firmly that "I can't really say I had any problem with discrimination."

CLO

In 1988 Ayo's room-mate at Law School suggested that to celebrate the Tenth Anniversary of their being called to the Bar they should hold a celebratory lunch. The news went round and on the day of the lunch thirty lawyers assembled, including Olisa Agbakoba, one of the founders of CLO (Civil Liberties Organisation). "He told me that I should come and help out. Then they immediately tried to corral me into the women's rights issues programmes, but I refused and argued that I wanted to be part of the mainstream programme. You know, people call me a human rights lawyer but I'm not, although I have always been interested in politics."

When CLO later decided that it needed a vice president, it was suggested that Ayo stand for the post, because she was so articulate at meetings. "As a lawyer I'm trained to say what's on my mind. I was elected by an overwhelming majority and I remember one lawyer told me that now that I'm in it, there was no turning back." This was the time when General Babangida was engineering the programme of transition from military to democratically elected government, "so I did not think I was putting myself in any danger – the military regime would soon be over and we would be back to democracy, right? Wrong! We all know what happened. But having put my hand to the plough I had to stick it out."

Soon Ayo recognised that it would not be possible for her to leave Nigeria because in 1996 her passport was confiscated. Then in 1998 the security forces arrested Olisa and brought him to the CLO office to search the premises. Fortunately for Ayo he managed, while the security forces were in the office, to alert one of the CLO members that Ayo's name was on the list of those intended for arrest. "I was told, I went home and the next day was planning to go to Court as usual." This could be considered to be either extremely determined and courageous or extremely foolhardy. The friend in whom she confided about her imminent danger was in no doubt. "He said that they can try to arrest me, but there was no reason to make it easy for them by sitting at home waiting for them to pick me up. Arrangements were made and I went into hiding. There I stayed for months until the sudden death of Abacha brought an end to the regime."

Family and career for women

When Ayo returned to Nigeria after her English education it was to discover that Nigerian girls "seemed to be obsessed with the business of husbands and the rest of it and it seemed to me that the things that they did were dictated by whether there would be a husband at the end of the day or not. I had no such motivations."

For Ayo it would have been simply too limiting an ambition. As far as she is concerned women have the right to work and to pursue their own careers and there is no question that the Law is a suitable profession for women. "It's not a matter of saying women can't do it, they are there. With time, there will be more women in Law School. The number keeps increasing all the time."

Mary Odili

Mary Odili is a judge in the Court of Appeal and is one of the founders of The Adolescent Project.

"I got into the habit of writing my judgments between the time when my children went to bed and my husband came home from hospital."

As she sat happily, relaxing after a successful session speaking at a Law Conference in London, Mary Odili reflected on the different strands of her life as judge, wife of the Governor of River State, Nigeria and philanthropist. And above all about hard work.

Fathers and daughters

The daughter of a Nigerian barrister, Eze Bernard Nzenwa, trained at Lincoln's Inn, Mary's reasons for becoming a member of the judiciary are to some extent shared by Dame Elizabeth Butler-Sloss, the recently retired President of the Family Division Court in the United Kingdom. Dame Elizabeth's father, High Court Judge Sir Cecil Havers, counselled her to accept the invitation of the President of the Family Division to become a Registrar in the Family Division on the grounds that it would enable her to spend more time with her husband and children instead of racketing around the country developing her personal practice. And it was Mary's husband, a newly qualified doctor, who suggested to her that becoming a Magistrate would be much more compatible with family life than private practice.

Because Mary was only 26 and had qualified as an attorney only 16 months previously, this would have been a surprising suggestion in the UK with its mandatory years of qualification requirement but Mary obediently, and one suspects with a convenient obedience, because Mary Odili does not look like a pushover for anyone, left the Ministry of Justice and joined the Magistracy to sit on the Bench as a sole presiding magistrate. But then she had been the best student in the Department of Commercial and Property Law in the years at the University of Nigeria.

Unlike Dame Elizabeth's father, Mary's father had not joined the ranks of the judiciary, because "he felt that in that role his personal character would come into play. He was an extrovert, he thought that he would not have the patience and also that he would not be able to sentence another human being to the punishments decreed by legislation." Instead he became Secretary to Nigerian Airways, the Chairman of the Nigerian Football Association, and more importantly eventually combined private practice with the position of traditional ruler of his part of Imo State in Eastern Nigeria.

Natural justice

As traditional ruler, his function was to act as a focal point for his people. This is particularly important when national or state governments may change frequently either through the democratic process or by military coup. To some extent he was called upon to dispense justice in a persuasive and 'natural' way and to act as mediator between his people and the government of the day.

Enticed by the external panoply of the law, "It was his wig and gown that attracted me when I went to see him in court," Mary was also encouraged in her ambitions by her mother, a successful businesswoman. "My father was always so busy that most of the time my mother was the one who paid attention to us; she believed in hard work and the right of all women to work for financial independence. Financial independence to enable them to take care of their families but also just for their own individual self-esteem."

The laws of inheritance

Her mother's good advice was very much influenced by the potential inequity of traditional inheritance laws in some parts of the country, which for centuries had required that on a man's death his wife and effectively his property, pass to his brother except where he has a male heir. In some parts of Nigeria the wife and children are not permitted to inherit any of the man's property which must pass to his nearest male relative and his children. In the mid Nineties one group of children refused to hand over their deceased father's property and were taken to court by "the uncles." This case was heard by Mary Odili, appointed a High Court Judge in Rivers State in 1992.

Her 1997 judgement was based on the clause in the Nigerian constitution which provides that "no child shall be disadvantaged on account of his birth." The children kept their father's property. "The problem has been that people are not familiar with the court processes, and so have not felt confident to argue against the inheritance traditions, but now more children are feeling confident about arguing for their rights." She adds quietly, with obvious pride, that many women lawyers give free legal advice in such cases, and that many judges are now protecting the rights of children to inherit their fathers' property. And she points out with equal pride that application to the courts to permit sons and daughters to inherit equally was granted by the Nigerian Court of Appeal in 1996 and endorsed by the Supreme Court in 1998.

The medical perspective

Mary's career both as a lawyer and as the wife of Peter Odili, a 'Rivers man' has made her not only aware of the difficulties of life for some in a modern African state but has also given her the opportunity to do something to help the less fortunate and the disadvantaged. After a post-qualification year at the Liverpool School of Tropical Medicine in 1985 Peter came back to Nigeria with the stark message "AIDS is real."

Up till then there had been a willingness to attribute the symptoms to other diseases and deficiencies under the pretence that there was not one overarching debilitating cause. With the stark new research information he brought back Peter Odili began a campaign to have the prevalence and even existence of AIDS recognised; Mary helped by attending the 1987 International AIDS conference in Harare with him.

The Adolescent Project

Her own legal experiences in close proximity with her husband's medical understanding have resulted in an informed determination to improve life for the people of her adoptive state. Although Port Harcourt is at the centre of the oil and gas extraction industry in Nigeria, the general populace of Rivers State is "one of the poorest in the country because of the terrain. Rivers State is deltaic and the populace have traditionally depended on fishing and farming on exactly those areas where the oil and gas deposits are to be found." Their livelihood has been destroyed either by pollution or through the simple loss of their land to the building of oil company buildings and refineries.

This has led to immense problems for the state's young people, "teen-age pregnancy, high drop-out rates from school, adolescent unrest." You can treat the symptoms through medical care or the results by incarceration, or you can as Mary has attempted to do, go straight for the root causes. Being 'First Lady of Rivers State' (her husband Peter became its Governor in 1999) helped her to gather other women lawyers and representatives of women's groups to discuss what was "practical and possible". The result was The Adolescent Project or TAP.

"I had a wonderful team who operated across many professional spheres" One of Mary's characteristics is that she takes very little obvious personal credit for what she does in the social sphere because she feels that "if a group works as a team it is difficult to fail" Together her team raised funds from multinationals, from state government and local government, from people from outside her state, in fact from anyone who could be persuaded to invest in the future of Rivers State's young people.

Reaching out to the Community

Mary's modus operandi is forward-looking and pragmatic. The team started with basic health education to prevent teen-age pregnancies and exhorted young people to remain at school. When they learned from a survey of young people that many of them were dropping out only because of family poverty, TAP also set up workshops to give women the marketable skills to pay for their children's schooling.

The unacceptably high perinatal and maternal death rate has been reduced by simply encouraging the 'traditional midwives' on whom the village women were dependent to attend two week training courses to learn about washing their hands, wearing rubber gloves, keeping their instruments clean and most importantly how to recognise which deliveries could have potentially fatal consequences without hospital treatment. Two weeks may not seem very much, even with the monitoring system set up to support midwives, but this elementary training has not only saved the lives of many mothers and new born babies but has, as a by product, given the midwives a status within their villages and prepared them to advocate the wearing of condoms and to give advice on AIDS.

Partly as a result of the TAP's team's influence female circumcision is now illegal in Rivers State and medically required deliveries by Caesarean Section are now paid for by the state and not by the patient. This latter piece of legislation is very important to Mary because the hypertension she suffered during pregnancy meant that all her four children were delivered in this way. Now she is a grandmother with one daughter who is a doctor, two daughters who are law students and a son who is studying medicine.

Of judges and judging

Mary says quietly that she "derives lots of fulfilment and happiness from her legal work," and she described in great detail the stages by which a junior lawyer may progress to the Nigerian Court of Appeal, as she did in 2004.

"Magistrates Grade 3 have the power to sentence only up to 6 months, Grade 2s may sentence up to 18 months and a Chief Magistrate may sentence up to 7 years," but from the beginning the new magistrate hears both civil and criminal cases.

Mary was appointed to the Federal Court of Appeal in 2004. Although appointment is made on merit, in recent years an attempt has been made, where all other things are equal, to reflect the geographical and demographic spread of Nigeria's population in Court of Appeal appointments. One surprising statistic is that although the Supreme Court, Nigeria's highest court has only one woman judge out of 17, 20% of Court of Appeal judges are women. Even more surprising is Mary's calm statement, as of a normal thing, that "in Lagos 54 of the 63 judges are women." Even if we accept that many of these will occupy the lowest rungs of Magistracy status this is still a surprisingly high proportion.

Mary ascribes this to the perception of the judiciary as a stable occupation with regular hours enabling women to combine a career with family responsibilities. Men on the other hand, perceive the lower echelons of the judiciary as insufficiently remunerative to enable them to provide financially for their families. As the route to the High Court appears to be as open to magistrates as QCs the welcome result is that there are likely to be proportionately more women judges in high places in Nigeria than in the UK.

Low salaries can of course lead to the possibility of corruption, but Mary has a very clear view on that. "I have always known how to look out for trouble. Some people do fall into temptation but because I did not do so as a young magistrate, and people recognised that, there is no expectation that I can be bribed now. People are comfortable with the fact that I am not going to be corrupted. Our

President is leading the battle against corruption very strongly, and Justice Uwais, when he was Chief Justice said publicly that the judiciary will cleanse itself."

Towards the future

Mary is very optimistic about the future and about the future of the legal system in Nigeria. There have been many regime changes during her judicial career, but succeeding governments have "left the judiciary alone. Our judicial officers have not had the same difficulties as judges in oppressive regimes. They were not jailed, thrown out of office or persecuted. The Government simply ignored some of their judgments, but left it at that." This may seem a surprisingly accomodating attitude until we remember that in some other African countries judges have been removed from office and attorneys beaten up for representing their clients against the governments of the day.

Mary's unhesitating advice to young women lawyers, that "they should give it their best but never forget that at the same time they have roles as wives and mothers," was the thought that propelled her into the judiciary half her life ago, but her influence extends much wider than her immediate family, to 'the team' which translates her charismatic enthusiasm into reality. "I have lots of associates involved, meeting me and advising me what to do, and many people participate in making things work. I have had lots of support and lots of enthusiasm from people volunteering to assist. My most important role is to encourage people, and especially young people, to feel that there is dignity in labour. And I couldn't persuade young girls if I were just a First Lady who went around in a lot of gold jewellery who had never worked and who had no understanding of their difficulties."

Justina Offiah

Justina Offiah served as Attorney General and Commissioner for Justice in Enugu State between 1994 and 1997 and in 2004 became the first woman from the South East to become a Senior Advocate of Nigeria (SAN).

A little over half a century ago Justina Anayo Iloeje was born in Nsukka, in Enugu State in Eastern Nigeria. She spent the first ten years of her life at home with her parents in Nsukka, but after her tenth birthday was sent to live with her eldest brother, a civil servant and a Lecturer at Government College, Umuahia, and when her brother was posted from Umuahia to Enugu and then on to Onitsha, all small towns in the old Eastern Region, Justina went with him.

Education and War

Even at this early age Justina's intellectual capabilities were obvious. She was accepted by Queen's College, Enugu, one of the best girls' schools in the country. As it was the only female Government College in the Eastern Region at that time, its limited places were highly prized. "It was exclusive in terms of the level of academic excellence required to gain admission there, and I feel that I had good teachers and a good education there." However, two years later, the Nigerian Civil War erupted between the Nigerian Federation and Biafra (as the breakaway republic was called) and for Justina this meant an interlude of thirty months when she received no formal education at all. Although the Biafrans tried to maintain their children's education by organising tutorial classes, the intermittent bombings and sudden evacuation of families in fear of attack made this almost impossible. "You would be at school to-day, but to-morrow you had to relocate because the place where you had been was over run by soldiers. Nothing was stable so we could not really have an education."

At the conclusion of the Civil War children were able to return to school, but "after the War a lot of things changed…not for the better." When the War broke out many people who had been displaced from the Northern and Western parts of Nigeria returned to the East. They had to be assimilated into Eastern society and systems, including the educational system. At the end of the War, most did not return to the North and West because of the continuing hostilities there, and this also exerted considerable pressure on the remaining schools in the East. Inevitably the War had resulted in another sort of migration. At the beginning of her education at Queen's College Justina found that her fellow students came from all parts of Nigeria, but during the War those who were not Easterners left, and they did not return. The educational disruption was not felt to the same extent by those of her class mates who had returned to other parts of the country and they were able to carry on with their education and to complete it ahead of their compatriots in the East.

On cessation of the hostilities the authorities attempted to compensate for the difference in experience and attainment by simply moving all the Eastern children up one class, "but we had to work extremely hard to cope. When I left school at the beginning of the War in July I still had six months of the academic year to go in Class 2. After the War I was simply put in Class 3. And I did not return to the same school. The buildings had been mostly destroyed, and the few that were left were dilapidated and damaged." School ended for Justina in 1972 when, like many of her colleagues, she sat the National Examination and the West African Examination at the same time. Her legal education then began at the University of Nigeria in Enugu.

Why Law?

Like many other lawyers, Justina's initial career interest was in Drama. At school she wrote short plays and poems, and was a leading light in the school dramatic society. Perhaps unfortunately for the stage, but certainly not for the Law, there were no career prospects for Theatre Arts graduates at that time other than in teaching, which Justina did not find attractive. She had to look for other options. "Now we have Nollywood (Nigeria's vibrant home video and entertainment industry, christened Nollywood after Hollywood in California and more recently Bollywood in India) but there were no dreams of Nollywood at the time." For a while Architecture was under consideration but rejected as she was not particularly strong in Maths. At this point of indecision she found herself sitting in a courtroom for no particular reason and seeing lawyers at work "suddenly caught my attention." She spent some time finding out about lawyers and what they did and "it dawned on me that these people had the ability and the opportunity to speak for people who could not speak for themselves. They were able to champion the unheard voices, and I realised that that was exactly what I wanted to do." Two of her friends who had lawyers in the family reinforced her first impressions, and Andrew Iketuonye SAN, Nigeria's 39th Senior Advocate, and the father of her friend Millicent, whetted her appetite for legal endeavour by taking the time to give her a further insight into the profession.

Private practice

At the time Justina started to practise, "there were a lot of cultural restrictions in our thinking, our philosophies were very culture bound and it appeared at the time that some professions were male preserves. There were very few women in the legal profession as our culture saw it as highly intellectual and beyond the capabilities of a woman. In my University year, 81 of us graduated, but not even 20% of us were women, and even that was a fairly large number of girls compared to the year before." When after Law School she returned to Enugu to practise, there were only four other women lawyers in private practice in the whole of Enugu at that time.

Justina had decided on private practice for two main reasons, one idealistic and the other more pragmatic. First because of the dream she had of speaking for the voiceless, which was an ambition supported by her family. "The background in my family was such that you had the opportunity of full self expression in your career." Second, during the compulsory chambers attachment while at Law School Justina had been given the opportunity of working in the Chambers of Chief Mogboh SAN and that experience had ignited her passion for advocacy. At the end of the attachment period the Chief had also effectively offered her a place by remarking that "if after your Law School you want to be a lawyer, feel free to come back."

So eager was Justina to embark on her new career, that when she concluded her Law School training, she returned to her home state, dropped her bag at home and went straight to Chief Mogboh's Chambers. "Chief said, "Are you back?" and I replied, "Yes," and he said, "Welcome back, this is your file for Monday." I have been there ever since … twenty seven years now."

It was a vibrant chambers with a varied number of cases and Chief Mogboh, the Principal, was "like a father, mentoring and training, whilst giving you the opportunity for self expression. There were no specialist areas and the chambers dealt with all areas of litigation. You had to have the ability to work hard and you had to be trustworthy or you would have no place in his chambers. Once you displayed the willingness to work and to learn, he would guide you and teach you all that you needed in order to develop and to get job satisfaction out of what you did." To some Justina might seem singularly unworldly as she indicates that it was certainly not the promise of riches that drew her to the Law and to private practice. "We did not discuss money. It was not my primary interest at all. I did not discuss salary or payment or allowances or anything of that nature. It was never discussed. To date it has never been discussed. I just wanted to learn Law and to practise and I was determined to do just that. Whatever came as remuneration was left entirely to his discretion but I can say that I have always had sufficient to meet my needs, I did not lack anything. He was very fair."

A woman in a man's world

Justina started in practice as a "spinster" and married shortly afterwards. During the early days, concerned male colleagues, and even other women, told her that private practice was too strenuous for a woman. Some of her subsequent experiences might have justified their pessimism, but Justina has always felt that her commitment to her profession and to its ideals would carry her through its difficulties. She recalls with a hearty laugh one elderly lady from her home village who was astonished to learn of Justina's new profession. Horrified, she asked, "Justina, is it right that your job is to stand and speak in public? You children of nowadays!" In her opinion Justina had chosen to throw all shame and decorum to the winds and her behaviour was scandalous and totally lacking in modesty.

Justina was well aware that even in the Seventies the traditional maxim that "women, like children, should be seen and not heard," was still very powerful. She was told time and time again that she would not be able to cope, and when this assertion clearly did not change her behaviour or affect her success, the comments were expanded to "What does your husband say? Does he not mind?" Justina received all sorts of unwanted advice about the effect that her cross-country travelling as an advocate to represent her clients would have on her family life. She was even asked such pointedly personal questions as "Who cooks in your house?"

Male attitudes

Justina feels an immense gratitude towards her husband, who "has been wonderful and so supportive. He is a medical doctor and working very long hours himself and being so committed to his patients, he understands my commitment to my clients. Between us we were able to juggle our lives and to manage the children. Yes, we had to sacrifice some things, social life for instance, but then we would rather spend the time with our children." The comments about her lack of decorum, the physical demands the job would place on her as a woman and the possible effects on her family life "somehow did not discourage me too much." As far as clients are concerned, "their prejudices did not last too long, because clients come to chambers and see you at work and also see you at work in Court and they develop confidence in your abilities. In fact after one or two appearances they are comfortable with your skills and your coming to Court with them. Having their matters handled well is what they really want, and if you succeed in doing that, some of them will soon ask for you specifically to represent them."

Justina's colleagues initially adopted an attitude of genuinely concerned surprise that she was there at all. "They felt for me as a woman. How would I cope?" But over the years, by continuously dealing with any difficulties and showing that she could work as hard as any other lawyer, and by not letting down the Chambers' clients, Justina proved her worth, so that ultimately whether or not she could "cope" ceased to be an issue. In Court it could be a different matter. When she began there were very few female judges or magistrates, so male judges and magistrates often did not see women lawyers on a day to day basis. Justina did not have any difficulties within her own immediate jurisdiction where she became a familiar figure in Court, but in other jurisdictions, where some of the judges encountered no female lawyers at all, "there was a lot of doubt as to your ability and you had to prove yourself." Generally speaking Justina found that the Bench was very encouraging, provided that "they see that you have a zeal and a drive and you are making the effort. Even when you make mistakes, they are not impatient and sometimes they help you and guide you with suggestions. "Well have you looked at this provision? Would you like to address me on this?" And gradually you pick up what you should be doing. But anyone who was not making much of an effort, whether male or female, was given very short shrift!"

"I do not recall any occasion where my client was prejudiced simply because a woman was presenting the case. However, there may have been cases where cultural bias affected the judgement given for or against my client, not because she was represented by a woman lawyer, but simply because she herself was a woman. Cultural norms and beliefs can be very powerful."

Family and time-tabling

In order to cope Justina learned to put a clear dividing line between "my domestic affairs and my professional affairs. I did not take home files and I did not make up my shopping lists in the office. When I am at home, I am a wife and a mother and I mind my domestic responsibilities, and when I am in the office, I am a lawyer and I deal with my clients." Although she admits that she had house helps from the start of her career, "I organised things in such a way that they did what they had to do and I did what I had to do. The trick is to delegate and then supervise. You do not delegate and then abandon." And once again Justina points out how supportive her husband has always been.

Making everything work requires meticulous organisation, for the responsibilities of motherhood (Justina has six children) are not suddenly lifted because a woman is an effective and highly regarded lawyer. Justina is usually up by 4.15 am for prayers, shower and then Morning Mass. "I am a Catholic and I like to start the day with Mass. I then come back and help out with preparations for breakfast. When the children were younger it was more tedious because sometimes they decided that they wanted to eat something else, or indeed nothing at all, but somehow we managed." School runs were shared between Justina and her husband depending on their individual schedules and also with their neighbours. Justina preferred the morning run "as I could not always predict the day in Court and some afternoons I might be out of town for a case." Again her commitment to both her profession and her family is obvious as she describes the way that she plans her day to fit round both. "I was in Court every day except for holidays like Christmas. When the children were younger, I would finish my work at Court, go home to be with them, and then return to Chambers about 4.00 pm to finish at whatever time was necessary to conclude the job in hand. After they got older I was able to work through the day." She does not say whether this meant that she was able to finish her working day any earlier!

Just getting about

The physical aspects of life as an advocate, let alone the intellectual ones, hard for anyone, are especially testing for a woman. "It was not easy," Justina says simply. "I remember some of the journeys I had to make to get to the Court. I travelled from Enugu to Ogoja sometimes, a journey of over eight hours by dusty very bad pot holed roads and would arrive all dusty in the Park (where interstate vehicles loaded and dropped off passengers). If I was lucky there would be a taxi to take me to the guest house where I would spend the night reading and preparing for the hearing the next day. If I was not lucky, then I just picked up my case (which invariably weighed a lot because of the books) and trekked it the four or five miles to the guest house." As Justina describes this travel uncertainty, she is not formulating a complaint but simply making a matter of fact statement about the real life of an advocate. "You are driven by the case and you just have to do what you have to do to get the case done."

In 1983 Chief Mogboh, Justina and some younger lawyers were dealing with election petitions being heard by the

Electoral Tribunals. The time constraints involved were very stringent and Chief Mogboh's Chambers had received a great many briefs from one of the political parties. The Chief had to go to the Supreme Court then in Lagos for the famous *Onoh v Nwobodo* case, which concerned a dispute as to who had been validly elected to the Governorship of the old Anambra State, and Justina was left to deal with the cases in the local area. The schedule she adhered to sounds particularly severe for a woman who was at that time expecting her third child. "The cases started in the morning with the witnesses, you then put in the evidence, took a break for lunch, prepared your address, rendered your address and the Tribunal gave judgement. The days were very long, and one night we finished at about 12.15 am and I immediately left Nsukka to begin the two hour journey back to Enugu by road to get home because I had to be in court the next day at Abakaliki (two hours by road the other way) for another election petition."

Life in Court

From the work that she has done over the years Justina has derived great professional satisfaction, particularly when matters have gone in her client's favour. There have also been frustrations, "such as those moments when you have arrived in court fully prepared and ready to proceed, only to have the matter adjourned. Equally frustrating are those rare occasions when the judge simply does not follow your line of reasoning, and it feels like you are talking to a wall."

Justina is still disturbed by one particular case where she felt that there had been a miscarriage of justice against her client, a woman, because of cultural chauvinism which blinded the judge to reason. The judge ruled that the matrimonial home of the woman was the village or ancestral home of the husband and that she was therefore not entitled to a share of the house in town where they actually lived and for which she had contributed a large share towards the building costs. As the town house was not regarded as the "matrimonial" home and it was in the husband's sole name the judge felt able to deny the woman's request for a share. The husband was an interstate truck driver on a small fixed wage while his wife engaged herself as a petty trader. The evidence showed that she earned the higher income of the two and so must have contributed more, but none of this was taken into consideration because of the decision based on traditional cultural norms that the city home could not possibly be classed as the matrimonial home.

Becoming an SAN

The conferment of the title of Senior Advocate of Nigeria must be the peak of the career of any Nigerian lawyer in private practice. "I have to say that this has been a high point for me. Quite a journey up. The legal profession was a man's world when I started and women coming in were like interlopers, but gradually that began to change" Aiming for SAN status has been one of the challenges in Justina's professional life. She says regretfully that "many women have been burnt out along the way, some gave up practice and others went into the Ministries or in-house. Not many stayed in private practice, although in theory the opportunity is there for everyone." Substantial tenacity is needed for any lawyer to have any chance of success and also a certain degree of luck. An advocate aspiring to this highest accolade must have been involved in the "right kind of cases. You have to have at least four Supreme Court judgments to your credit in any number of three years preceding the application, and of course some people, even in many years of practice, do not have even one case at Supreme Court level because it really depends on the type of matters they deal with."

Now that Justina is an SAN she is offered the most fascinating and challenging briefs and in common with QCs (Queen's Counsel) in the United Kingdom she can more or less name her fee, although, she stresses, fees are no more a motivating factor for her now than they were when she first set out as a junior in Chief Mogboh's Chambers.

Geraldine Ekanem Oku

Geraldine Ekanem Oku was a lecturer at the University of Calabar, in-house Counsel for a Nigerian bank in Lagos, and most recently has set up her own training consultancy.

Geraldine Ekanem Oku, or "Jerry" as she is popularly known, is a woman of complexity and strength of character. Her elegant appearance easily combines the modern (beautifully groomed hair and light make up accentuating her classic bone structure) with the traditional (a vividly coloured ankle length caftan or boubou covers her slim figure.)

Geraldine was born in Lagos, the eldest child of an unusually small family by African standards. She has a younger brother, who lives in England and a sister who lives in Nigeria. Whether her parents had ideas of the future direction of their daughter's life when they gave her the middle name of Ekanem it is difficult to say. The words which make up the name and the essence of the name could be said to mean "being a mother is a good or joyful time," but Geraldine's life was to take a different more independent course.

Early life and education

Geraldine's father was a successful architect and home was in a quiet estate in Apapa, inhabited mainly by the last few colonial civil servants still working in Nigeria at the time. "We were one of the few black families living there." Life in Apapa was peaceful and safe and there were few opportunities for childhood mischief. As everyone knew everyone else the estate grapevine ensured that parents would have heard of any childish pranks on the streets long before the culprits arrived home. Her father's strictness coloured her relationship with him and it was not until her mother's relatively recent death that she drew closer to him.

Her last year in Corona Primary School, Ikoyi, a genteel school in one of the more exclusive suburbs of Lagos, coincided with the end of the Nigerian Civil War. Her parents decided to return with their young family to their native city of Calabar in Cross River State in the southern part of Nigeria to participate in the rebuilding of the city. The transition from the quiet expatriate estate in Apapa and from Corona Ikoyi to the city of Calabar which, though serene and green, was recovering from the ravages of the civil war, was potentially traumatic. In Lagos she had not been much affected by the Civil War whereas the education of most of her classmates in her new school had been severely disrupted. Consequently "I found that most of them were much older than I was. However, some of the friends I made then at Holy Child School are friends even now."

Holy Child, Calabar, which Geraldine attended as a day student, was "an excellent mission school" run by nuns. With a smile she pointed out that boyfriends were totally out of the question and that her understanding of men and their expectations was gleaned from the numerous Mills & Boons novels she devoured in her teenage years. But then all was change again. After excellent O Levels and a year of A Levels at Hope Wardell, Calabar, Geraldine was sent off to England by her parents to give her exposure to a more international experience. Already half way through her A Level studies, Geraldine was unhappy with this decision, but at that time no well brought up girl would have thought of disobeying her parents' wishes, especially if, as in this case, both parents had themselves studied in England.

A rebel for Law

There were no lawyers in the immediate family and far from encouraging her to study Law, Geraldine's father wanted her to study either architecture as he had done, or failing that, medicine. "But I am a bit of a rebel, and I do still like my independence."

It turns out that the decision to study Law was the result of a bit of a muddle. Law was not in fact her first choice career. Initially she applied to study English Literature and Language at the more traditional English universities. The application process took a long time and Geraldine became impatient for something to do. She followed a friend's advice to apply to the University of Buckingham, a privately funded English university which operates on a different term system, to study Law. The friend argued that studying Law there would give Geraldine something interesting to do while she waited for the results of her applications to the other universities. By the time (only a couple of months later) that she was given a place to study Literature at Queen Mary College in London, she had discovered the fascination of Law. The place at Queen Mary's was turned down and two years later Geraldine graduated with a Law degree from Buckingham.

This first degree was followed by a second, a Masters degree in Company Law and related subjects, such as Marine Insurance, at University College, London, which she combined with a diploma in French. By the time that she had finished her studies there she was "completely captivated by the Law." She was also becoming aware of her capacity for hard work and diversity of application. Indeed she felt "fantastic" that she had been able to combine her Masters degree with the Diploma in French despite "always having to run from one class to another." Fortunately her father had become reconciled to her career choice and although he could not attend her graduation, sent a letter saying how proud he was of her achievements.

But why Law?

Following a career in the Law was the right course for Geraldine because she "liked the intellectual independence I gained from studying Law. It suited my nature because I hate to be told what to do and I like to think my own thoughts and learn from my own mistakes." In her view it is also a good tool to reach out to other people, to educate them and even to influence them positively.

The Law is a house of many mansions and the ultimate aspect of the Law which suits any one individual lawyer may not be immediately obvious. Geraldine is clear that "I didn't go into the Law to make lots of money," but she did not know at the beginning that she would be commercially minded. Not knowing what prospects there were in Commercial or any other area of Law when she was making her choice of Masters subjects she simply fixed on those subjects that she found most interesting. At one point she was attracted to Criminal Law but was put off after watching an autopsy in progress while learning the law of evidence. And the concern that she could become too emotionally involved led her to reject the thought of practising Family Law. "I simply could not see myself as a good Family Lawyer."

The pursuit of excellence in whatever she does is clearly important to Geraldine. She feels very strongly that the way a student is taught Law will determine how good a lawyer that student will turn out to be and will dictate how he or she practises. From the start Geraldine was taught to rely entirely on herself and her own research. It is her firm belief that the lack of handouts or lecture notes on her course helped her to develop the right attitude and skills from a very early stage in her career.

Back to Nigeria

Now armed with two degrees Geraldine returned to Nigeria where she taught Law for five years at the University of Calabar. Her teaching methods came as somewhat of a rude shock to her students who had become accustomed to lecturers preparing and handing out reams of notes. Instead she pointed out to her students that as lawyers they would be required to think on their feet. Therefore it was essential that they develop good research skills and a creative approach to Law and its practice. She was not prepared to spoon feed her students as she truly felt that this would be "detrimental in the long run and they just had to get used to it."

Her experience of honing her own research skills and explaining matters to her students with crystal clarity was put into practice when she decided to make the transition from academic to in-house counsel. This was quite a step, and her success in taking this substantial step makes her commentary on what a lawyer needs to consider in this process worth listening to.

Commercial requirements

First of all, she recommends, you should decide on the commercial sector in which you wish to operate, whether it is in banking, aviation or oil and gas, inform yourself not only about the law relating to that sector but also about the way that companies operate and make money within that sector, and most importantly about "how your chosen sector operates in this country." Then move on to detail about the companies in which you are interested, find out who are the members of the board, their backgrounds, qualifications, skills and achievements, as the make up of a company's board will impact very heavily on that company. Commercial in-house practice is ever developing and requires some knowledge of many different aspects of the Law such as Patent Law and Competition Law as well as basic Contract Law. Before taking an in-house position it is therefore essential to ascertain what training opportunities come as part of the compensation package. If none are planned you need to be able to negotiate a training package at an early stage and, most importantly for a commercial lawyer, ensure that the agreement is documented!

Geraldine is always aware of the human aspect of any particular situation. Acting for a company is not just a matter of being aware of the Law relative to the sector in which the company operates. "You need to be able to navigate your way round corporate politics without compromising your integrity." You must have faith in yourself, constantly ask questions, "be a nuisance in asking questions" be willing to get knocked down, then accept it and get up for the next round. To be of real value to the company you must develop a set of core values that you know are not negotiable and that you will not compromise for anything or anyone. And you must "continually update yourself" and continue to train because "there is nothing like knowledge and information."

As well as knowledge and access to information a keen practical intelligence for dealing with gender difficulties is also required. Although Geraldine considers that she has not suffered from any overt sexual discrimination, she has certainly received more than her fair share of "inappropriate" compliments and jokes which she generally ignores, and suspect invitations to meals and social events to which she gives a polite refusal. Discrimination is more likely to be indirect in the implicit requirement that women conform to the long hours macho culture in order to obtain promotion and advancement. In her view far too many meetings are unnecessary and overlong, stretching into the small hours of the night.

Having said all that, she admits that in her own world as in-house counsel to a bank, there is no "typical" day as each day brings a different set of challenges. There is however, a general pattern as most days start with telephone calls in the morning re-confirming appointments and meetings, followed by those meetings between 9 pm and 3 pm with the inevitable follow up work there after. Often she finds that her working day ends at 10 pm or 11 pm because of the need to fit round her clients' own working patterns.

Geraldine is very disappointed in those in-house counsel who describe themselves as "only in-house lawyers." They need to be proud of what they do, so that they can acquire sufficient stature within their companies to be taken seriously. This is not just a matter of personal pride but is essential for the smooth and legal running of their organisations. She realises that a lot of company executives may "do all sorts of things without consulting you, and then they expect you to perform magic to make everything go away or to make it alright." Geraldine points out that colluding in this type of request is very dangerous, particularly in the finance sector because the Central Bank of Nigeria comes first to in-house counsel as "you are regarded as the repositary of all crucial documentation in a bank.

So, where a bank starts to fail it comes from you as in-house counsel, not from the finance officer, but from you."

Strength of character is therefore necessary for in-house counsel, but training in real corporate governance should also be required of bank chief executives and directors so that they will realise how important it is to "respect their in-house counsel and support them."

Hard work

Geraldine is not sure whether she made a deliberate choice not to marry, but feels that she was certainly "just taken up by a very high pressure career." Such total involvement would not be the route for everyone, but for Geraldine with her background of high standards, energetic dedication and belief in doing the best possible for others it was perhaps inevitable. Finding herself as "usually the only woman in top management," in business situations certainly, produced a lot of pressure "working with men, particularly Nigerian men."

This has resulted in a life where she "usually works at weekends, even during the night, because the way that business is done in Nigeria is often very unstructured." What she very much wants to find for her clients is a solution to their difficulties. She strongly believes that "where there is conflict, there is resolution, and I apply that to matters of the Law." This maxim is bolstered by a pragmatic understanding of the reality of Litigation.

Litigation in Nigeria, as in other countries, is "costly in terms of time and energy" both for the client and the lawyer, and then in the end, particularly if you do not get the result that your client wants, your client may simply not pay your fees. Consequently young lawyers should be trained to realise that the practice of Law does not mean "that you fight every time." Geraldine feels encouraged that in Nigeria "we are beginning to wake up to ADR (Alternative Dispute Resolution), particularly mediation, which encourages most of us to actually resolve our problems by ourselves rather than by using arbitration."

What is success?

As a practising Buddhist, a faith to which she was introduced by her sister, this is a question which she has considered carefully. Success in her view is "not a holistic thing," but is rather something that we need to aim for in each individual day of our lives. It is not something to be measured in material terms, but "I measure success in terms of fulfilment, your own personal fulfilment as a human being." It comes from having a positive impact on other people, and indeed what you have done one day "may not register on your consciousness, but if you have succeeded in doing something for that day, then you will look forward to the next day."

"I believe we are all in this world to be happy and to help others to be happy. If you are not happy, then you are not a success. I don't care how much money you make, how much property you have, if you are not a happy human being, then you have failed. My challenge is to continue to be successful and not just in terms of a profession or career, but in terms of using that profession or career to impact positively on other people's lives. My profession is a tool not an end."

But inevitably there have been individual high points in her career to date. Her appointment to the Privatisation Council of her state following the national move to privatisation in 1999 required confirmation by the State Legislative House, as this was a huge undertaking affecting about 1,000 state-owned companies. Part of the confirmation process required her to appear before the House of Assembly where she was once again the only woman among men. "I was taken last but I refused to feel disrespected." She was then asked a series of detailed questions by one of the Assembly men "about my background and all that." After a time the Speaker of the House intervened. "Why are you asking all these questions? You know as well as I do that she taught two thirds of us in this hall." "I was so honoured," she recalls, "and felt very humble" that her former students would so readily vouch for her integrity.

Success is also intrinsically associated with learning, the acquisition of new skills and experience. This was certainly the case when she was involved in the raising of funds by a bank client for the building of a road round the key business areas of Nigeria. To finance the project, funds had to be solicited from many European countries as well as the United States. The Central Bank of Nigeria required a specific level of capitalisation within a tight time frame and Geraldine was proud that she assisted her client to exceed the investment target by a considerable amount. Managing a project of this size and complexity made Geraldine realise that she had "some skills I didn't know I had" such as marketing and computer skills and also the ability "to force the banks to knuckle down and do the work that they should have done." The latter skill one would suggest is simply a characteristic of all good teachers.

Women and careers

Geraldine has no doubt that she found in Law the ideal career to utilise her enquiring mind, her dedication to assisting others and her capacity for hard work. The skills she has acquired as a lawyer have, she believes, equipped her to fulfil her mission in life and have given her a sense of self belief which she would not have derived from any other profession.

Law she considers is not only a suitable profession for women, it is almost crucial for women to study Law. There are several reasons for this. A career in the Law more than any other imbues one with leadership qualities, and historically those women who have had the most influence have had legal backgrounds. "Studying the Law opens up your consciousness to your rights and the rights of others; women have nurturing qualities and so tend to come out batting on behalf of others far more than men would."

In fact "we have excellent women in Nigeria. A lot of us don't believe in ourselves and I think that we need to come out of the shadows and make the impact that is needed to enable Nigeria to burn all the brighter."

What of the future?

This image of "burning brighter" is clearly in tune with Geraldine's own future destiny. Will her life and career continue along the same path into the future? This is not totally likely. She sees herself in five years time possibly operating in a slightly different field, that of "public service," service to the community rather than to individual clients. But what exactly the nature of that service will be, we shall simply have to wait and see.

Yinka Omorogbe

*Professor Yinka Omorogbe is the Dean of the Faculty of Law of
the University of Ibadan. She is also a Chartered Arbitrator,
a consultant on Energy Law and Policy, a member of the Oil and
Gas Reform Implementation Committee, Managing Director of the
Centre for Petroleum, Environment and Development Studies and
the General Secretary of the Nigeria Society of International Law.*

Education in brief

Yinka Omorogbe was born Yinka Ighodaro in Ibadan and
spent her early years there. After Kindergarten and the
University Staff School, Ibadan, she attended St Louis Girls'
School, a Roman Catholic school run by nuns, which Yinka
considers was "quite progressive and fairly liberal. We were
not expected to fall down on our knees every day at midday
to say the Angelus and neither were we made to go to Mass
every day, although of course it was compulsory on Sundays.
We had a nun who sang a lot and we all developed a love of
music and singing because of her." Yinka in fact learned to
play the guitar, which she still plays, and also the piano
which she studied to Royal School of Music Grade VI. She
sat her A Levels at the International School Ibadan before
gaining admission to the University of Ife to study Law.

Family background

Yinka has strong childhood memories of, and a great affection for Ibadan. "Those of us who know Ibadan well, all love Ibadan. It is a very hospitable city and an educated place."

She came from a family of "educational pioneers" where education was highly valued. Both her parents were professionals, appreciated the independence made possible by their professional status and were determined that their children should have the same advantages, although she and her three siblings were given a relatively free choice as to what subjects they would study when they eventually arrived at college. Yinka's mother had been not only the first woman to qualify as a medical doctor in Sierra Leone, her country of birth, but was also only the second woman to do so in the entire West African region. She was a member of the Wellesley Cole family and therefore among the first to benefit from Western education. Her brother Robert, Yinka's uncle, also a doctor, was the author of the African literary classic, "Kossoh Town Boy," which described Sierra Leonian city life at that time.

Yinka's mother was "extremely active," combining private practice with family responsibilities and community work. A founding member of the YWCA, the National Council of Women Societies and the Medical Women's Association of Nigeria, she was also involved in numerous other clubs and societies and undertook a great deal of informal mentoring and counselling. Always in private practice apart from a stint as Chairman of the University of Benin Teaching Hospital, she was passionate about issues relating to women and their circumstances.

When he graduated in Theology Yinka's father became the first citizen of the ancient Bini Kingdom to graduate from university, following this with another Bini first when he later qualified as a lawyer. While studying at Fourah Bay College in Sierra Leone he was introduced to the Wellesley Cole family, and to the young daughter of the family, Irene, who would eventually return to Nigeria with him as his bride and become Yinka's mother.

Actively involved in politics on his return to Nigeria Yinka's father S. O. Ighodaro joined the Action Party where he worked very closely with Chief Obafemi Awolowo, serving the emerging Nigerian nation first as Minister for Health and then as Attorney General of the Federation. He was later appointed a judge and served in the judiciary from 1968 to 1972 when he retired from active practice to take up the role of Iyase (Prime Minister) of the Bini Kingdom. In this role he was rather a novelty. He was monogamous, whereas Binis at that social level usually have several wives.

Why Law?

Yinka's natural flair for design and drawing led her first to consider Architecture as a possible career, but when the final decision on a university course had to be made she "fell into the Law," as the result of a conversation on a very long car journey with Chief Awokoya, a political friend of her father's. Up to that time she had been uncertain as to which university course to pursue. Her main criterion seemed to be that it would require the minimum exertion on her part, and when she got into the car had almost decided on English Literature as being interesting but not too demanding. This may be a limited ambition for a woman who has subsequently achieved so much, but as well as deciding on a university course she was also having to come to terms with having had her first child, a son, at the age of 16. Fortunately she had the support of both her parents and one wonders whether in fact her father who was clearly aware of his daughter's abilities (she admitted later that "I think I was a natural lawyer") had engineered the conversation with his friend.

In any event Chief Awokoya, who had served as Minister of Education in Awolowo's Government and had helped to bring about universal free primary education in western Nigeria, used his time well, and pointed out the many advantages to be gained from joining the legal profession. "And in the end I heard. My parents had said the same thing, but my home was a very individualistic one. In my home we were allowed to do what we consider is right," and as a result during that fateful journey she made a decision which was to shape the rest of her life.

Many Nigerian parents of that generation would have exerted considerable pressure on their children's choice of career, but the philosophy of Yinka's parents was "pretty much to allow you to make your choices in life so long as you could justify those choices to them." Through this strategy they succeeded in influencing her indirectly towards the career in which she has ultimately excelled. Wise parents!

University life

In 1975 Yinka was admitted to the Law Faculty of the University of Ife, subsequently renamed Obafemi Awolowo University. "The University was a very friendly and intellectually stimulating place" where lecturers and students interacted freely and exchanged ideas. Students were encouraged to strive for excellence although Yinka admits with cheerful self deprecation that she was not very studious and more or less coasted along without paying serious attention to her work.

After graduation in 1978, she proceeded to Lagos to study at the Nigerian Law School for the equivalent of the United

Kingdom Bar Vocational Course or Legal Practice Course. At the end of the one year programme, she was called to the Bar as a solicitor and advocate of the Supreme Court of Nigeria. The young female lawyer was soon employed in private practice in the chambers of Asemota & Co where she honed her advocacy skills by undertaking a wide variety of cases. She had a slight frisson of doubt about her future legal career but when she suggested to her mother that she might return to university to study Architecture the response was extremely unsympathetic. How could Yinka be so self-centred as to contemplate a change of career now that she had made her father so happy by choosing to study Law?

However, all her doubts disappeared when in 1981 she left Asemota & Co to undertake the LLM programme at the London School of Economics in the UK. When she discovered Energy and Petroleum Law her whole attitude changed. Her love affair with the Law which she firmly believes is an essential ingredient in every society, "the framework on which society rests," had finally begun.

Energy and economics

Her focus on Energy and Petroleum Law Yinka ascribes to the one teacher she found intellectually stimulating and interesting at the University of Ife, the late Dr Adeniji. His lively classes ignited her interest and she was soon fascinated by the subject. No other tutor at Ife inspired her in the same way, and in typical Yinka fashion she even refused to attend those classes she found particularly boring. It is a testament to her innate legal abilities that despite this she performed creditably well in some subjects and outstandingly well in others.

For her LLM programme Yinka chose to study International Law, International Economic Law and Armed

Conflict together with a fourth course undertaken in the form of a project supervised by Rosalyn Higgins, now the current President of the International Court of Justice, but at that time a Visiting Fellow of the LSE Law Faculty. The pleasure that she obtained from writing this project was the beginning of her life long interest in research. Indeed so influential was Lady Justice Higgins on her future academic life that Yinka opines thoughtfully that she was perhaps the only real female role model she has ever had.

Yinka's passion is the international legal scene, "I find the international legal system far more interesting than the municipal law system," but she would not now exchange any aspect of a legal career, which she considers herself fortunate to have found. It is easy to speculate that if she had opted for Architecture she might have been responsible for outstanding new buildings in Lagos and Abuja rather than the training of outstanding new lawyers for the Nigerian legal system. There is however no doubting her solid belief in the rule of law and in the vital role that lawyers must play in civil society as "we are the bedrock of society. A good society is dependent on framework. Good law should be effective and invisible, once it becomes visible and obtrusive then it is bad law and should be amended."

Yinka believes that there is room for improvement in terms of standards in the legal profession but reflects gently that lawyers are a product of the society in which they live. If standards have deteriorated generally, then it is likely that lawyers' professional behaviour will also reflect that. This should not however be regarded as an adequate excuse for poor performance as individuals themselves can resolve to set themselves a higher standard and to make the necessary sacrifices to meet this higher standard.

Women's place in the Law

Any question as to whether the law is a suitable profession for women is to Yinka perplexing because unnecessary. She clearly does not think along gender lines in terms of her profession and is extremely surprised that anyone else might. In her opinion any profession is a 'suitable' profession for women, and women should pursue whatever interests them in the same way as men. However, they should be aware that if a profession becomes 'feminised,' as the nursing profession has, by valuing mostly traditional female skills and being occupied mainly by women, it will lose its value in the eyes of the public. "We have to accept that life is harder for women, so we just have to work that much harder. I do admit that studying for me was not difficult and I do have a great capacity for work and work very hard indeed. Any woman who wishes to succeed has to understand that this is an essential ingredient of success. If you are bright but innately lazy, you will not succeed whilst a hardworking person with little ability can certainly become successful. I admit to some advantages as a result of my background but this only makes it slightly easier and is not essential for success."

Although Yinka admits that at some points in the past she has suffered from discrimination she is not certain whether this was as the result of her gender or was the consequence of her own non-deferential and outspoken demeanour. She takes such questions seriously and responds with carefully chosen words in measured tones when she relates her own experiences. She said that there was an expectation in Nigeria that subordinates would behave not just in a respectful manner but that they would be subservient in a "sufficiently humble way. There's an extra special sort of bending that you have to do in the presence of your boss. It is a fact of life in Nigeria and I think that people who don't might sometimes suffer unless they have people who are tolerant around them." Yinka stooped her shoulders in a servile manner to demonstrate very graphically what she meant. "I was not able to do this and I may inadvertently have offended some people with my lack of what they thought of as 'respect'." This is a very interesting observation on her part as it shows just how important a knowledge of cultural expectations can be when it comes to getting on in professional terms.

This difficulty was most acute when she was a lecturer in the University of Lagos Law Faculty. She was denied promotion for twelve years and was eventually involuntarily retired at an unprecedentedly early age. (Even now she is still only in her fifties.) She was given no explanation for this action but accepted her fate with good grace. Fortunately for Nigeria, the decision was reversed and she was recalled after twenty two months in the academic wilderness.

What happened to Yinka has been the common experience of those women who are the first to enter the legal profession in whatever country they live and work. Male lawyers, judges and academics have often acted as though female lawyers and students are covered with a cloak of invisibility.

Yinka is not bitter about her experiences but sees them as the source of amusing anecdotes. Once at a conference where the delegates were, as is pretty much the norm in her field, predominantly male, she put her hand up to ask a question. The Chairman of the session studiously ignored her while giving various male delegates the opportunity to air their views. To the intense amusement of the delegates around her, mostly male officers of a certain rank in the Nigerian Navy, this culminated in the Chairman calling the man immediately behind her to speak while apparently being totally unaware that Yinka was still waving her hand in the air. One of the officers commented ironically that perhaps her hand was simply too small and slim to be seen. After the session she asked the Chairman why he had so pointedly ignored her. His response was that he thought that she was putting her hand up on behalf of the man behind her; it was therefore very reasonable to by pass her and to call on the man directly. As far fetched as this seems the Chairman was probably speaking with absolute candour, convinced that his actions were reasonable when he gave this explanation, but "of course he would not have made this assumption if I were a man."

Hard work

For Yinka there is no such thing as a 'typical' working day as the shape of any day is dictated very much by the particular set of tasks in hand. As Dean of the Law Faculty, she shoulders a huge administrative burden usually dealt with in her Faculty office. In order to maximise the efficiency of her time there she tries to arrange related appointments to coincide with office based days; in this way she manages to confine all administrative matters, including responding to correspondence, to the times that she schedules for the office. Any serious research or writing is done at home in the relative quiet and seclusion of her study, and legislative drafting work is carried out in the early hours of the morning or very late at night when she is able to concentrate with absolutely no distractions.

It is inevitable that the breadth of Yinka's commitments will often produce very long working days, which may begin at about 8.00 am and end with winding down at about 10.00 pm. She commutes over state lines, travelling from her home in Lagos to the University of Ibadan campus on a regular basis, and a long day in Ibadan or an early start may entail spending the night in her official accommodation provided by the University authorities.

Family life

The appearance of her pretty daughter clad in a night dress and a sleepy smile prompts the question, how does she juggle these long hours with a family life involving a husband and three children? Yinka comments with a wry smile that she had earlier said that women had a harder life. When her children were younger she would help the children with their homework first, listen to their accounts of their day and then put them to bed before returning to work until the early hours of the morning.

Unwinding at the end of the day involves even more reading, but perhaps harking back to her once 'idle' thought of studying English at university she enjoys modern novels as well as philosophy and books on self development. The Argentinian novelist Isabella Allende is a particular favourite, but she also reads widely among African writers including the younger generation of writers such as Sefi Attah and Chimamanda Adichie, the author of 'Purple Hibiscus.' Television is watched only if "I happen upon an interesting programme," although her daughter states categorically that she is not good at watching television as she does not get passionate about any of it and finds most of the programmes entirely forgettable.

Reflecting on life

Yinka sees her career in terms of a continuum of progress rather than a series of high and low points, "but if there is such a thing as a high point, it would be when I became a

Professor" as she had been denied this for so long and at one point did not think she would ever achieve it within the Nigerian academic system. "It may also be because it is viewed as the apex of an academic career by the general public." It is also an important point in that other people realised that "I was as competent as I believed myself to be."

"But then," she adds, "for me there's no sense in doing something and not getting to where you're going. But then it's a stepping stone to greater things." As far as the Law is concerned "if you like it, do it. If you don't like it, then run away. I don't see any point in doing anything at which you are not likely to excel. It's good to try to excel."

It has not been easy to attain the levels of competence and recognition that she has achieved to-day. Clearly endowed with natural intelligence and a formidable capacity for hard work, the greatest challenges in her long career have been less personal intellectual than external physical ones. The lack of research materials and the spasmodic electricity supply were the greatest hindrances to her progress in learning until she was in a position to supply both from her own resources. She is also very grateful that she has been able to utilise the NNPC Library and also materials available through the International Bar Association Section on Oil and Gas.

Having learned at an early stage in her career that she could not depend on the poorly funded colleges for vital research materials, Yinka has gradually built up a large private library at home. The cost of doing this was less than might be imagined, she points out, because she was "a bit of a pioneer as regards Nigerian Energy Law, so I dealt with a lot of original documentation. It was more of leg work, detective work, real research work with original data." The advent of the Internet has in her view revolutionised access to information from the perspective of a researcher, but she still feels that it would "be good if we could have great libraries in the country."

And what else?

In common with many other successful people, (and it should be noted that "being a bit of a pioneer" meant starting the first Energy Law course at the University of Benin on her return from London,) Yinka finds time as well as fulfilling her academic duties, carrying out her consultancy work and conducting arbitrations to get involved in wider community issues. She assists with community outreach programmes such as 'Christ Against Drug Abuse' which provides practical assistance and counselling to drug addicts and other victims of substance abuse.

Of the media coverage of her work with patients in the Igbobi Orthopaedic Hospital in Lagos she explains simply, "we have been going there for fifteen years to see these patients and to do what little we can for them. Initially they were twelve paraplegic patients for whom the hospital and medical science could do no more but who could not return home either because they had no homes or no relatives, or because the burden of caring for them would have been intolerable for those relatives they did have." When there were only three patients left, the hospital authorities stated that their beds were required for patients whom they could properly assist.

When she read about this, Yinka realised that "it was tantamount to a death sentence for the surviving three as they would simply have been abandoned to die." She wrote to a few friends telling them about the plight of the patients and asking them to help to fund the construction of a bungalow in Spinal Cord Village (a part of Lagos set aside by the Government to house people with spinal cord injuries who may have been abandoned by their families or whose families simply cannot cope with the burden.) Within weeks a bungalow had been erected to which the three patients were relocated together with an accompanying fanfare organised by the hospital's director, no doubt keen to show the general public that they were not as heartless as they may have been portrayed in the media and that it had all ended well.

The real instigator of this happy ending, Professor Yinka Omorogbe was content for them to take the accolade. .

Amina Oyagbola

Amina Oyagbola is Corporate Services Executive of MTN Nigeria and also Executive Director of the MTN Foundation.

Amina's office is on the eighth floor of an imposing office block enhanced by floor to ceiling glass windows, which give breathtaking views of Victoria Island, Lagos. Her office is simply furnished with one stunning piece of African art taking centre stage above the uncluttered desk, behind which Amina herself sits dressed in a simple yellow boubou, inadvertently living up to her name as "the y'ello lady."

A travelling education

Because her parents were diplomats Amina had a very peripatetic education in the early years of her life, moving from primary school to primary school (spending only two years in Corona School, Ikoyi) until she and her brother were "deposited" in public schools in England. Consequently she completed her secondary education at Kent College in Pembury, Tunbridge Wells. "This was a wonderful time in my life." She was appointed Co-Head Girl – the first black girl in the school to occupy that position.

After A Levels her father decided that the best thing for her would be to go to university in Nigeria, because, as he said to her mother, "these children have spent too many years abroad and will probably never go back home if we do not make them come home now." Amina had "a passion for History and that was what I had applied for at school in England," but her father insisted that she needed a profession. "He said it would give me more versatility and scope. I was easily persuaded and I decided to follow my father's advice." Although there were lawyers in her extended family, this in itself had no influence on the decision that led to her spending three "glorious" years at Ahmadu Bello University in Zaria studying Law. She graduated with a 2:1 in 1982 and was also awarded the prize for the best graduating student of her year.

Going to Law School meant she had the "exciting" experience of discovering Lagos, where her parents were now living. This was also where she met her husband Bayo, who, after graduating from University College, London, had returned home to Law School in Nigeria. After Law School Amina served her NYSC at Bonny Camp (a military base) where the work was varied and interesting, including dealing with courts martial, because "the culture in the army is entirely different from the culture in civilian society. I met some very nice people whom I am still in touch with today."

She recalls with a smile that it was a really wonderful time of her life when both she and her husband were serving their NYSC in Lagos, as she was "starry eyed and very much in love." At the end of the NYSC year it was back to England to study for postgraduate degrees in Law. Amina obtained a Masters Degree at Trinity College, Cambridge, and this time when they returned to Nigeria it was to settle down, if such a thing is really possible for Amina's enquiring spirit, to professional life in their native country.

Apprenticeship

Amina has always been conscious that she comes from a "privileged" background, and did not want to use this to gain an undue advantage when looking for her first real position as a lawyer. "I did not want to be seen as someone who had been given a job for reasons other than merit."

It is this concern that no one should accuse her of taking advantage of nepotism that made her relate carefully the process that led her to the Chambers of Chief Rotimi Williams. As a result of working hard for them during the compulsory chambers attachment in Law School, Kehinde Sofola & Co "recommended me to someone who managed to get me an interview for Chief Williams Chambers." Despite performing well before a panel of three senior lawyers, Amina was "absolutely gutted" to learn that they could not offer her an immediate start at this stage, "although they said they would keep me in view. You see I did not have a plan B." But when he discovered what had happened, the uncle of a friend then "took it upon himself," she emphasises, to draft a formal appeal to Chief Williams asking him to reconsider Amina's application. The stratagem worked and after five years working with Chief Williams, "I realised that it was probably because he was so tickled by this approach (as he had a wonderful sense of humour) that he had reconsidered and had invited me to start work immediately."

As a young lawyer she earned very little money, but felt that she was in the best possible place to learn and grow. "Chief Williams was a great mentor, he gave all his lawyers the latitude to find themselves as individuals both intellectually and otherwise and he always used to say "the world is your oyster, you can make of it what you want". The opportunity was there, we had a beautiful library and the books were there. If you wanted to be laid back and not grow, he would not push you, but if you wanted to learn, he would invest the time to teach you and encourage you. We called his wife "mama" and she was there for us too with lunch every day after court. We would sit around the dining table with Chief at the head and we would have lunch together. Every day we would discuss our cases and what had transpired in court and we would raise any issues and discuss what we called "small points". Chief never made anyone feel too small. He made us all feel we could contribute something and he opened up the vista for creativity and created an environment which enabled learning and generated ideas and that is something I have taken away as a life long lesson."

What happened next?

This was, Amina thought, the ideal place to spend the rest of her legal career. However, her father drew her attention to an opportunity with one of the new generation banks. Somewhat reluctantly she went through the recruitment process, but the letter from Crystal Bank of Africa offering her an income package of more than five times her current earnings was tempting enough for her to go to Chief Williams for advice. To his credit Chief Williams encouraged her to "try out the corporate world," assuring her that there would always be a place for her at Rotimi Williams & Co if it did not work out. Emboldened by that assurance, Amina took the leap into the corporate world as an in-house counsel.

Amina joined Crystal Bank of Africa in 1990 and very quickly found herself with an ever-expanding portfolio.

From the ideal family world of Rotimi Williams & Co she was thrown into what felt like the "Wild, Wild West" of legal affairs. For the first time she encountered boardroom politics. The six years spent at Crystal Bank, which later became Standard Trust, opened her eyes to the realities and not just the theory of business life, and she credits her experience there as a fertile training ground for all that she currently does with MTN.

Crystal Bank

Amina very quickly grew beyond being "only a lawyer." At one point, she was asked to set up a branch office in Ikeja with the promise that, "we will give you the basic training in credit and accounting and what ever tools you need." She soon realised that this meant finding a building on Allen Avenue for the Bank, renovating it, negotiating with the architect, ordering all the equipment and fittings, recruiting all the staff and taking full charge of the branch, "and as there was no customers, I had to then go out and get them. As a matter of fact, there was very little law in what I was doing, but I think it was the legal grounding I had behind me that gave me confidence and enabled me to do it successfully. Somebody had faith in me and was ready to take a chance on me. I was able to build the balance sheet of that branch from zero to over two hundred million naira in less than a year and was able to sign in a large number of corporate accounts. It was wonderful exposure for me."

What she had not realised up to that point was that the kind of thing that was going to give her real satisfaction was working hard to start something from nothing and completing it successfully to realise a vision. It was invigorating, challenging and enjoyable and building up a team was satisfying. "I had a strong unit head who was in charge of operations, a strong unit head in charge of marketing and altogether an excellent team, so that from the HR perspective, the consumer perspective and the marketing perspective it was all very successful."

Unfortunately it soon became clear that in the period whilst she had been dealing with the challenges of the Ikeja branch she had lost touch with what was happening in the Crystal Bank organisation as a whole. She realised that "things were not going in the right direction and that was when I decided to leave. One piece of advice I would give to others is that you must not bury your head in the sand. You must have foresight. Don't sit down and wait for things to happen. I had seen the signals, read the signals and I said to myself this doesn't bode well and I don't want to be here when things fall apart. So I tidied my books and made sure that every credit facility I had given was returned and handed over neatly."

This aspect of Amina's character of "being prepared" and alert not only got her out of Crystal Bank, but ensured that she was ready for the next challenge. But where was she to find it? And would the first offer be the best offer?

Getting a new job

Within a week of sending her CV "which I always had ready online" to a professional recruitment company she had received a job offer from another new generation bank which she decided to accept.

"Life is very interesting. It's true that Man proposes but God disposes. When I look back over my career, it was not designed by me, my only contribution in all of this is that God has given me the strength to work hard and endowed me with intellect. I don't think I am the most brilliant person around, far from it; I believe I have above average intelligence, but do not consider myself to be a wiz kid. You know you come across some people who naturally pick things up just like that. (She snaps her fingers to illustrate the point) I don't put myself in that category at all. But what I do have, that many people don't have, is determination, industry, dedication and organisation." In her view being intellectually brilliant may not be enough in itself to guarantee success. "Sometimes all that talent and knowledge comes so naturally to clever people that they feel they don't have to work or be focused, but in real life, you'll find that it is the people who get up and go, who take action and who are ready to work hard, who will really stay ahead."

Having made the decision to accept the offer from the new generation bank, Amina went out to dinner with friends, and fortuitously met the Executive Director of Management Services at the United Bank of Africa (UBA). As he was someone she knew well from Law College, conversation naturally covered their careers since then, and when he realised she was in the middle of a career change, he asked her to send him her CV. He spoke glowingly of all the changes that would shortly be happening in UBA and of the Bank's intention to begin a radical transformation. "And he said to me, you are just the kind of person that we need. More out of courtesy than any real desire to go to UBA I agreed to send him my CV."

"My husband has always been an excellent counsellor and adviser to me, so when he encouraged me to go for the interview which the UBA Board had set up for me, I went." His advice was sound and resulted in Amina being offered a position and a remuneration package even better than the offer from the other bank, "and that was how I ended up in UBA as the Principal Manager and Number Two in the UBA Legal Department. It was yet another wonderful opportunity.

We transformed the former Legal Department completely. We equipped it, changed the orientation, put new processes and procedures in place and turned it into a professional corporate legal department in line with international best practice. We streamlined the Litigation portfolio, had some very interesting transactions going through the bank and I really loved it."

In less than a year, Amina's boss was elevated to the UBA Board and she became the Head of Legal. This gave her the opportunity to set up a series of annual lectures, inviting the Attorney General and other legal luminaries to speak; even Chief Williams came to deliver a lecture. "It was a really good, very vibrant, and a lovely legal department with capable specialists. We ensured there was good governance, no corruption and no chopping money from external counsel. We tried to be a role model, to show corporate Nigeria how a legal department should really be run, I was very proud to be part of that work."

All change again

After about two years when the reorganisation work was complete and everything was going well, Amina told her team that they had effectively made her redundant. "I think that there are certain people who are driven and who constantly need to take up new challenges. There was nothing more for me to do there."

This led her to a radical reassessment of both the organisation and of her own abilities. She realised that although she had acquired a substantial knowledge of the banking sector and considerable general management skills, she would always be pigeon-holed as a legal specialist, unless she acquired some new skills to enable her to progress professionally. "So I decided that I needed to broaden my horizons and the best way to do it was to get an MBA." But there was a problem with this grand idea. "I knew I didn't have the money, and I wanted to go to one of the top schools. Fortunately someone told me that the British Council might offer a scholarship, so I applied, went through the interview and I was privileged to be granted a Chevening Scholarship. And that was how I came to go back to England for a year to undertake the MBA programme at Lancaster University Management School."

Amina narrates this as though it were a fairy story. "And that was how I came to go abroad again." Perhaps that is exactly how it felt. "It was like a whole new world, a whole new experience, a whole new framework of concepts, mental and moral, and it was such a glorious challenging year. I thought I was going to die at one point, it was so hard. Many times I asked myself, what are you doing here, but in the end it was worth the money, all the time and all the sacrifice."

Many happy years

Amina is fulsome in praise of her husband's support, understanding and ambition for her. He it was who encouraged her to go to the UBA interview and he did not hesitate to push her towards the MBA adventure when she hesitated. She was after all a married woman with three children. "However, he encouraged me and insisted that he would be able to cope with the kids with the support of other members of the family, my parents and my sisters." This is yet another instance of the importance of the extended family to the success of talented women in Nigerian society. "Sincerely I could not have done it without them."

Amina makes the next step in her career seem very simple. She took very seriously the advice given on the course that it would be wise not to return to the same professional position when the course had ended. "Others may not realise that you have changed but you will have changed dramatically." At a recruitment fair in England she made contact with Citibank who asked her to contact their Lagos office. "That was what I did." This resulted in her being offered the position of Deputy General Manager of Citibank Personal Banking.

But Amina felt constrained to return to UBA to ensure that she left without undue friction. "I owed it to my supervisors in UBA, they were very good employers, so I told them that I would like to work out a suitable notice period to ensure minimum disruption for the organisation." Amina now had a new dilemma because UBA exceeded the offer from Citibank. An intense session with her husband followed, and after conducting a SWOT analysis of her options he advised her to remain with UBA.

His advice resulted in "many happy years" at UBA but eventually the time came once again when she felt ready for new challenges and began to look at industries outside the banking sector.

Industrial focus

"So," she says with a mischievous smile, "I sent my CV to MTN," who were looking for a General Manager. Soon negotiations began in earnest on the benefits package. While these discussions were going on, fate again took a hand and postponed her future relationship with MTN. A chance meeting at a hairdressing salon one afternoon, with a friend she had not seen for some time, led to a discussion about working in the oil sector, and most particularly with Shell, where the friend was employed.

Fortuitously "a new position had just been created and my profile fitted it almost exactly." While in charge of the UBA Human Resources Department Amina had been sent on an

SAP Solutions payroll software course in South Africa, and it turned out that for Shell (SPDC) this was a considerable attraction. Shell also fitted Amina's requirements. "I loved my Shell experience even though it was very challenging. They have an excellent employee value proposition and invest heavily in training and developing their staff. I thought I would end my working career in Shell."

But change came again. "The invisible hand of God was at work again." As part of its restructuring strategy SPDC decided to shut down its Lagos office in order to focus on Port Harcourt and Warri. Knowing that family commitments would make it very difficult for her to leave Lagos, "I sat down and I said God, here I am again, because I didn't know where else to look. I just sat and prayed. Well, I was sitting in my office thinking all of this when I got a call from MTN." There was a vacant position, things were "really moving quickly" because of the appointment of a new Managing Director who wanted to assemble his own team very rapidly. "And so I ended up here, and it has been a good move. It is new, fast moving, empowering, vibrant and pioneering in many respects and extremely challenging. There is also the challenge of cultural differences, which you always need to adapt to. The South African approach may be different from the Nigerian approach, which may differ from the English one etc. But there is richness and strength in diversity. It has therefore been a very enriching experience for me so far. I have learned and I'm still learning new things every day in this fast growing industry called telecoms"

In the public eye

Amina is very proud of being the "public" face of MTN, which "is the biggest brand in the African mobile telephony market," and exhilarated because "anything that happens in

MTN is news." In addition to all the legal work, she has responsibility for governmental affairs, regulatory matters, corporate communications, both external and internal, and oversight of the company's secretariat, and she is also in charge of MTN's corporate social responsibility through her position as the Executive Director of the MTN Foundation that was set up just before she joined the company. Indeed one section of her office is very proudly devoted to all the awards won by her organisation.

Even in the supermarket, people approach Amina because she is often on television "trying to create awareness of one programme or another, not because we are trying to showcase what we are doing, but because we want to share the model and the process we have embarked on with other people so that they can emulate them and touch more lives."

The Foundation focuses on three areas; health, education and economic empowerment, which is a very broad set of aims in a country as large as Nigeria. In the area of education The Foundation is in partnership with UNICEF to help enhance the learning environment in primary schools by improving physical infrastructure, sanitation facilities and learning materials, and in partnership with SchoolNet to support secondary schools through the provision of computer laboratories to help bridge the knowledge and digital divide. This has now been done successfully in 37 schools in 9 states. The Foundation is also equipping universities with full digital reference libraries. On the health side, the Foundation has together with partners embarked on an HIV & AIDS campaign to provide awareness programmes, counselling, care, support and treatment for cases where HIV can be transmitted between mother and child. "This has led to our producing a documentary about our awareness campaign which we shall be sharing with other Nigerian companies, and also physically locating touch screens at strategic points with information on AIDS in the 3 key languages as well as broken English."

"This is a very meaningful part of my job. I have a passion for it, I just love to put a smile on the faces of people whose lives were touched. Contributing to socio-economic development is something my organisation and the Foundation Board takes very seriously. I see myself as holding and managing the funds in trust and I am therefore committed to ensuring that the funds are efficiently deployed and reach the beneficiaries."

Amina makes it very clear that doing this sort of work is beneficial to all. "The benefit for me is that it has also opened my eyes to Nigeria in the real sense. I now have a better understanding of the socio-economic issues and of how Nigeria actually works. As someone from the private sector, I can now better understand the public sector point of view, I can pick up the civil society angle because of the work that we are doing in the Foundation. I attend seminars and give lectures on corporate social responsibility issues. It is something I am really passionate about because it has meaning and can help to alleviate poverty and aid development."

"I want people to begin to challenge corporate organisations and to ask them what they are doing on the corporate social responsibility front. How have you helped to improve the lives of those around you, how have you been able to empower people and what real contribution have you made to society beyond being a good corporate citizen?"

Women in the Law

Women have made many serious advances in the legal profession in Nigeria, and Amina feels that they could advance further still if they get well organised. "I think we should develop strong female networks and support each other. That is what men have over women, they know how to network and know how to use the network to their benefit. Men know how to support each other professionally in the advancement of their careers and that is something women need to develop."

Career women in her view need to realise that to be successful requires focus, commitment and hard work. "I will do anything to support women but I also have very high expectations of them. I am therefore extremely hard on them and will not accept sloppy or incomplete work. They must work at organising themselves, so that they don't have to make excuses or disappoint supervisors who are relying on them to deliver. That is the way real life is. You have to decide whether you want to pursue a career and do all it takes or prefer to dedicate yourself to the family."

To succeed "you have to decide on what is important to you and focus your attention and energy on those things you consider a priority and then face the consequences that go with it." Lawyers have a great responsibility to their profession and to their country. "I think more professionalism is required in legal practice but I think that you cannot isolate legal practitioners from the society in which they live, I think that would be unfair." Legal training in her view gives its students one unique strength. "The profession is based on the ability to analyse and problem solve. Whatever the challenge, difficulty or uncertainty, lawyers have the ability to analyse, bring clarity to and work out the issues. That is what legal training provides. This is a skill that is invaluable in every facet of life; and I know I wouldn't have been sitting here today but for that grounding."

Her legal training has also given Amina an enquiring

mind and a desire to learn new skills. Life for her is a constant journey in the mould of Robert Louis Stevenson who said that "to travel hopefully is a better thing than to arrive and the true success is to labour." Amina has "stopped worrying" about the future and what comes next. "You can never see what is around the corner. I just thank God for the opportunity he has given me. From all of these organisations that I have worked in and the diverse and wonderful people I have met along the path, I have learned a tremendous amount and I am still learning, so what I do next I really don't know, but I think God will decide that in his own time as he always does."

Sally Udoma

Sally Udoma is General Manager, Executive Staff and General Counsel of Chevron Nigeria Limited. She is also Management Sponsor of the Chevron Nigeria Women's Network.

Sally Udoma lives in a house which is an ideal mix of all that is beautiful in African and European culture, very much like Sally herself. African motif cushions covered in black and white are carefully placed on black leather settees, the side tables have African images carved down the front of each leg and the mantel piece holds African vases of different sizes.

This theme is carried through the open plan and spacious living area to the dining section with its beautifully carved African chairs – Sally is clearly proud of her African heritage.

Early days

Sally was born in Yaba to a professional family, where her father was a lawyer and her mother was a qualified teacher. She recalls the years growing up in Yaba as happy and carefree. Children were allowed to go out and play with minimal supervision and would stroll from one suburb to another without fear at a time when Lagos was much smaller and had not lost that community spirit which is so difficult to retain when a city reaches mega status. She remembers how the sweet seller at the corner of her street knew them well and would often give them a few sweets as little gifts. She undoubtedly felt very safe as everyone knew everyone else.

Primary school started in Corona Yaba, which at the time was located within the military barracks. After the first military coup the soldiers locked up the barracks and Sally was moved to the University of Lagos Staff School in order to complete her primary school education. After a time at the International School in Ibadan she left for England and a Quaker run school in Saffron Walden to study for her A Levels.

A woman in the Law

"It was not my burning ambition to become a lawyer," Sally points out, but lest one should suspect undue pressure from her father, she states that her father's being a lawyer influenced her only to the extent that she had a good idea what it meant to work in the legal profession. For some time she also considered, but finally rejected, the idea of taking a degree in languages. The study of the Law she found intellectually challenging because "it stimulates independent and analytical thinking." Perhaps because she was so motivated by her studies she completed her Law Degree in record time and returned to Lagos and the practical part of her legal training at the Nigerian Law School. After her NYSC year as a youth corper, she became in-house counsel to Elf Petroleum Nigeria, which enabled her to spend 2 years in Paris improving her already fluent French as well as learning about corporate life, and has worked in-house in the Oil industry ever since.

Although Sally cannot recall any overt acts of discrimination which would prevent her achieving the status she now has within the corporate law arena, looking at her career to date objectively she argues that being a woman can sometimes be a hindrance and sometimes a help.

On the negative side she admits that she has on occasion had to argue for the same employment benefits as her male colleagues. In one instance Sally was not automatically given the right to the company housing to which all employees of her rank were entitled. Instead she was asked to provide a letter of permission from her husband confirming that the company was permitted to give her a house. As not one of her male colleagues was asked to provide an equivalent letter from his wife, she stood her ground until she obtained equal treatment. Occasionally, on the other hand, being female may have a positive impact because "male adversaries are more restrained and polite than perhaps they would be were they dealing with a fellow man. They have to hear you out because it would be rude and so they make that extra effort to be courteous." Sally adds acutely that perhaps there have been other instances of discrimination "that I simply have not noticed because I was not looking for them."

In-house activities

In Sally's working day which usually starts at about 7.30am, there would certainly be little time to search for the discriminatory behaviour of others. As she works for a company whose head office is American, the day starts with "a whole load of emails waiting to be answered." Chevron Nigeria Limited has "a significant amount of communication with the United States and the time difference means that most emails from there arrive during the night." During the day she might also deal with representatives from the Government and the Nigerian National Petroleum Corporation (NNPC) in addition to attending internal meetings and supervising her junior colleagues within her department and also the twelve other lawyers within the company.

Occasionally she attends meetings with law firms who want to introduce their firms for referral, but a great deal of her time is spent writing on the computer, giving written advice and responding to emails.

Winning a difficult case is always a cause for celebration. About ten years ago Chevron lost a very difficult arbitration, and Sally considered that the Arbitral award was "bizarre." Chevron appealed and won but the other side was very dogged and the matter went all the way to the Supreme Court until Chevron's position was upheld and they were vindicated.

Inevitably, as with any job, there are frustrations in being an in house lawyer, so she advises that it is very important for all lawyers, whether male or female, to assess their own individual strengths and weaknesses before applying for an in-house position. Mainly it is essential to recognise that the job will involve less legal work because much more time will be spent either on administration and supervisory/ political relationships or dealing with Government and third parties on issues that are not strictly speaking legal. "But," she considers, "if you enjoy the wider involvement in business matters, or being involved in the relationship between government and business, then being an in-house counsel could be immensely rewarding." Certainly working for an oil company in Nigeria contains much of the latter type of work.

Sally emphasises that gaining entry to in-house positions is not an easier option than working in private practice. "To come in as an in house lawyer what you need first of all is a very good first degree. Unfortunately with the intense competition that there is in Nigeria nowadays, really without a 2.1 you are not going to get into one of the better companies. You will of course require your professional qualification as well. Having a couple of years experience in practice first would also be an advantage. I didn't have that, but then that was some time ago, and I honestly think that those who do have some experience before entering commercial practice do have an advantage."

One of Sally's responsibilities is ensuring employee diversity in Chevron's Nigerian operations. Thus she is the Chairperson of Chevron's Diversity Council and has delivered a paper at the annual conference of the Nigerian Institute of Personnel Management on Diversity and Inclusion in the Workplace. But she does not see this merely as a matter of conferring rights to employees. Inclusion really means that people of all ages, ethnic origins, gender and religious persuasions should feel comfortable working together. And this is why, on Independence Day, Chevron holds a charity football match in which one of the teams, which consists of employees of all ages, religions and ethnic origins, both male and female, is proudly called the Sally Udoma Giants.

A legal recommendation?

It is essential in Sally's view, that those engaged in high pressure work whether legal or more general should learn how to relax effectively. She relaxes through a mixture of physical activity (swimming and going to the gym) and more cerebral pursuits (reading, but not work related reading!) She does not feel the need to belong to any wider and external women's group as Chevron has a woman workers' network of which Sally is a sponsor and member. And in any event, as the mother of three children, this is probably enough for any woman.

However, she is unhesitating in her recommendation of the Law as the possible basis for a fruitful career. "It gives you a lot of options because you do not have to be straitjacketed into anything. For example, we have lawyers in this company who work in Securities, in Supply Chain Management or in Human Resources. In fact it is really a very good training for life." Again Sally points out how important it is to be aware of your own personality traits and intellectual inclinations when opting for Law. "You do need to be someone who enjoys reading and thinking and analysing. You have to be somewhat analytical to succeed. Then, once you have qualified you must also consider carefully which aspects of professional activity you enjoy most, so that you can try to focus on directing your career in that area. For example, if you are able to talk confidently in public, you may want to go for Litigation, but even then there may be other things that you enjoy more."

Her advice to younger women thinking about going into the legal profession, "Don't be afraid to show initiative – take it wherever you can. Keep updating your skills, learn new skills and be confident. And never allow yourself to be intimidated by anybody."

It is certainly worth listening to what Sally says about the legal profession, as her husband is Senator Udo Udoma, a partner in Udo Udoma and Belo-Osagie, which has offices in 3 Nigerian cities, and her father-in-law was the first African Chief Justice of Uganda. So she has been able whether at first hand, or through close observation, to experience many different aspects of the legal profession.

Careers in the Law for Women

Background

The Nigerian legal system brought into being in the Nineteenth Century was originally based on the English common law legal tradition. The first attempt to regulate the practice of the legal profession in Nigeria was made in 1876 when the Supreme Court Ordinance was passed. This empowered the Chief Justice to admit and enrol as legal practitioners in Nigeria those who had been admitted to practise as barristers or solicitors in the various jurisdictions of the United Kingdom. There was also a facility to admit to practise as attorneys those who had acquired a sound knowledge of the Law acquired by close contact with legal practitioners in Nigeria.

There was one very substantial difference between the system in the United Kingdom and the system in Nigeria. Legal practitioners in the United Kingdom are either barristers or solicitors, and cannot practise as both at the same time. Crossover between the two branches of the legal profession in the UK is possible, but in order to become a solicitor a barrister must renounce her right to practise as a barrister, and a solicitor wishing to train as a barrister must give up her status as a solicitor. However, the initial shortage of legal practitioners in Nigeria meant that this separation of the branches could not be maintained, and this gradually led to a fused profession where Nigerian lawyers were required to operate as both solicitors and barristers.

An attempt in 1945 to regulate standards by requiring that only a person who was entitled to practise either as a barrister or solicitor in the United Kingdom could be admitted to practise in Nigeria was not entirely successful. Undoubtedly they had been well trained in the legal skills required for practice, but their effectiveness was hindered because they had been able to qualify as legal practitioners without knowing anything about Nigerian customary laws or sharia law, the personal law of a large portion of the population. Many also found it very difficult to combine both aspects of the profession.

This unsatisfactory situation ended after independence from colonial rule in 1960, when the first Law Faculty in Nigeria was established at the University of Nigeria, Nsukka, in 1961. This was swiftly followed by the University of Lagos in 1962 and Obafemi Awolowo University (the former University of Ife) shortly afterwards. When the Ahmadu Bello University, Zaria, was founded in 1962 it also included a Law Faculty.

Nigerian Law School

At the same time that Nigerian universities were offering LL.B degrees for the first time, the Council of Legal Education was established. Its primary responsibility was the training of prospective members of the legal profession in Nigeria, and in 1963 it established the Nigerian Law School to provide practical training for solicitors and barristers. It continues to be the body responsible for the accreditation, control and management of legal education in Nigeria.

Legal education and training in Nigeria is thus in two parts, the academic stage to be completed at a recognised university and the professional stage which is undertaken at the Nigerian Law School.

When in 1963 the Nigerian Law School opened its doors in Lagos, the then capital city of Nigeria, its first intake consisted of only eight students. More recently in March 2001 the Law School was decentralised and its headquarters moved to Bwari in Abuja, the new Federal Capital Territory. Now the Law School has four campuses. As well as the campus at Bwari there are campuses in Victoria Island, Lagos, in Kano at the former Bagauda Lake Resort and in Agbani, Enugu State, which is known as the Augustine Nnamani Campus.

The four campuses are headed by Deputy Directors General who report to the Nigerian Law School Director General, and have three academic departments, Litigation, Commercial Law and Commercial Practice, and Legal Drafting and Conveyancing. As all campuses run the same courses and offer an identical syllabus, it is probably geographical convenience which dictates students' choice of learning environment.

Law degrees in Nigeria

The first step towards qualification is to obtain a degree from a recognised university and the Council of Legal Education sets down stringent guidelines as to the courses and facilities which the university must provide before it will recognise the degree awarded as sufficient for entry into the Nigerian Law School.

The Law Faculty itself must have a separate and well-stocked Library facility away from the University's Library; it must contain relevant Law text books, local and foreign Law reports, statutes, journals and periodicals. There should also be a separate faculty building which can accommodate offices for the Dean and Lecturers and provide classrooms and other physical facilities. Common rooms for both staff and students, a moot court room and indoor and outdoor sporting facilities are also required. And most importantly, the faculty should have a sufficient number of qualified and experienced academic staff, including a Dean of Law of Professorial Grade.

The Academic Programme must cover the designated Core Subjects of Nigerian Legal System, Law of Contract, Law of Tort, Constitutional Law, Law of Evidence, Criminal Law, Nigerian Land Law, Equity and Trusts and Commercial Law.

The Law Faculty should be located in an environment which is conducive to the teaching of Law and the preparation of students for the final stage of their training at the Law School. Even if all the required facilities are in place the number of students admitted into the first academic year should not exceed 40, and only the specific quota of students approved by the Council of Legal Education for the Law Faculty will qualify for admission to the Nigerian Law School.

Entry requirements for the Nigerian Law School

The educational requirements for entry differ depending on whether the student concerned has obtained her first degree in Nigeria or in another country.

If the degree is obtained in Nigeria, it must be a Law Degree which has been awarded by an approved university, and a list of such universities may be obtained from the Nigerian Law School. For the purposes of such approval, the Council of Legal Education will have regard to the contents of the courses leading to the degree with a view to ensuring that the subjects taken and the depth covered are such that will provide the minimum basic knowledge of the Law as is required to enable a student to derive maximum benefit from the Nigerian Law School course, and ultimately to set up in legal practice in Nigeria.

If the degree is obtained from a university outside Nigeria, the accreditation of that university to the National Legal Professional Association in the country concerned will be considered. Only universities in common law countries are approved and only degrees awarded by a university to its internal students are recognised.

In addition those who have passed either the English, Irish or Scottish Bar Finals Examinations or those who have passed the English, Irish or Scottish Solicitors Finals Examinations will be accepted. (There have been alternative routes to qualification in these jurisdictions other than through first obtaining a Law Degree.) However, they must first study for and pass the Nigerian Bar Part I Examinations in Nigerian Legal System, Nigerian Land Law, Nigerian Criminal Law and Nigerian Constitutional Law.

All students, whether educated in Nigeria or elsewhere must then study for and undertake the Bar Part II Examination. This is the more practical part of a Nigerian lawyer's legal training and consists of courses in Civil Procedure, Company Law and Commercial Practice, Criminal Procedure, Law of Evidence, Legal Drafting and Conveyancing, Professional Ethics, Legal Practitioner's Accounts, Law Office Management and a General Paper.

Right to practise

The right to practise as a legal practitioner in Nigeria is regulated by the Legal Practitioners Act 1975 (now Act Cap. 207 Laws of the Federation 1990.)

A legal practitioner is someone who is "entitled in accordance with the provisions of this Act to practise as a barrister or as a solicitor, either generally or for the purpose of any particular office or proceedings," and such a person will be entitled to practise as "a barrister and solicitor if and only if his name is on the roll." The only exception to this requirement is where in accordance with S.2(2) of the 1975 Act, the Chief Justice of Nigeria by warrant authorises any person upon proper application to practise as a barrister for the purpose of particular proceedings described in the application. It is a mandatory requirement that the applicant must have been entitled to practise as an advocate in a country where the legal system is similar to that of Nigeria.

On successful completion of the Bar Part II Examinations students may apply to the Body of Benchers, the Governing Body of the Council of Legal Education, for Call to the Nigerian Bar. Each applicant must be sponsored by two Benchers as being a fit and proper person to be called. After the Call, students must then proceed to sign the Roll of Legal Practitioners in the Supreme Court before they can become eligible to practise. This means that they are then qualified to perform the functions of both barrister and solicitor in Nigeria.

Exemption

In certain limited circumstances it is possible for someone to qualify as a legal practitioner without undertaking the Law courses at the Nigerian Law School. This is possible if the applicant:

• is qualified to be admitted to the Law School; and

- has passed all core subjects prescribed by the Council of Legal Education; and
- at the time when qualification for admission to the Law School was obtained, or at a reasonable time thereafter, the opportunity to do so was lost for reasons beyond the applicant's control; and
- at the time of the application for exemption has satisfied the Council that the applicant had acquired knowledge and experience over a period of at least 5 years, sufficient for enrolment and that it would be unreasonable, having regard to all the circumstances, to require the applicant to go through the Law School; and
- has been attached to chambers approved by the Council for a period of at least 6 calendar months and completed all dinner obligations; and
- is a Nigerian citizen.

Once the Council has been satisfied on all these points it will issue a duly authenticated certificate exempting the applicant from the requirement to go through the Law School.

Practice

Once qualified legal practitioners must pay an annual practising fee to the Nigerian Bar Association in order to be granted rights of audience in court or to be permitted to prepare any legal document or hold any office as a legal practitioner. The Nigerian Bar Association is the professional body of legal practitioners in Nigeria, representing their interests and dealing with disciplinary matters.

There are many opportunities for lawyers in Nigeria, whether as in-house counsel, as Government lawyers, in academia or in private practice. Newly qualified practitioners should think very carefully about the area of legal life to which they would be best suited. This is not something which should be decided solely on the basis of potential earnings. Physical location, proximity to family, temperamental inclinations and academic interest are all equally important.

Even before a student qualifies she should be considering the course of her future career very carefully, although any decision made at the time of qualification need not be final. It is important to consult other lawyers and to ask them what they find irksome as well as fulfilling in what they do. Students should ask themselves whether they enjoy travel or whether they want certain working hours, whether they enjoy advocacy or whether they prefer quiet study, whether they enjoy negotiating on their clients' behalf or whether they prefer drafting. None of these activities is "better" than any other, but it is very important to understand yourself and to form some idea of what will make the Law a satisfying career for you.

For female lawyers there is often the added consideration of family and the need to create an appropriate balance between family and professional life. It is useful to discuss this with other senior women lawyers and to see what systems they have put in place to assist them, and what has been most helpful. To get the most out of any career in the Law will certainly require dedication and hard work.

Although lawyers in Nigeria operate as a fused profession, legal practitioners in private practice conduct themselves much more like UK barristers than UK solicitors. In reality the training is akin to a barrister's training in England and up to now lawyers have tended to think of themselves as being self employed rather than in partnership, with the result that they contribute a portion of their earnings to cover chambers expenses rather than share both expenses and income as is customary in a partnership. This can be hard on women taking maternity leave or attempting to work part-time as the amount required to cover chambers' expenses may form a disproportionately large part of their earnings. However, this is slowly changing, and more arrangements similar to solicitors' partnerships are emerging.

Senior Advocates of Nigeria

For those Nigerian lawyers who specialise in Court work, appointment as a Senior Advocate of Nigeria (SAN) is the acme of recognition by their peers. In order to achieve this distinction engaging in litigation is imperative. Appearance matters, although in this context appearance means the number of times that an advocate is heard in the Higher Courts from the Federal High Courts through the Court of Appeal to appearing in the Supreme Court.

The regulations for SAN appointment are under review and the committee charged with the task of reforming the entry criteria had not concluded at the time of publication. At present there are three qualifying categories, graded in alphabetical order from "A" to "C".

"A" represents those candidates who are the most qualified and who are short listed before the other two categories. The "A" list comprises those applicants who have had a minimum of six appearances at the Supreme Court in the preceding three years.

"B" list candidates have had at least two Supreme Court appearances and four appearances at the Court of Appeal level. "C" list candidates have had a minimum of two appearances at High Court level and four appearances at the level of the Court of Appeal. Interestingly applicants do not need to have won their cases; showing that they have conducted the matter to its logical conclusion by way of a judgement is sufficient whether or not the judgments were in their clients' favour.

Other aspects of an individual's practice are also taken into consideration, such as the number of lawyers in the practice. No fee is presently payable upon application although this is likely to change following the recommendations of the Review Committee. The names of the short listed applicants are circulated to all Supreme Court Justices, Justices of the Court of Appeal and the Chief Justice of each State High Court for their recommendations. The list is also sent to the President of the Nigerian Bar Association for his comments as he is required to confirm that he has no adverse comments to make on the applicant.

As a prerequisite to qualifying as an SAN a lawyer must have a minimum number of years of practice experience in addition to all of the above. Currently this is 10 years, but with the additional proviso that the applicant must have achieved excellence in advocacy and maintained it for that period.

It should be noted that it is possible for an academic lawyer to become a Senior Advocate of Nigeria, but that the application requirements would differ from those required of a legal practitioner in private practice.

More recently, and presumably in the spirit of welcoming Nigerians in the diaspora who return and to assist in re-integrating them into the fabric of the home country as soon as possible, Nigerian qualified lawyers who have already been appointed Queen's Counsel in England are automatically accorded the distinction of SAN.

It has been argued that the current system is flawed as it does not take into account the opinions of any lay persons and there are those both within and outside the profession who feel that the opinions of lay persons should also be canvassed. The selection process has also been criticised in some quarters because of a lack of transparency and there is also concern that the "appearance" requirement might encourage unnecessary litigation. It is thought that some lawyers may be tempted to persuade clients to appeal against a judgement in order to achieve the requisite number of appearances in one of the higher courts. The lawyer's personal interests in such a situation might then be in conflict with the best interests of the client.

These criticisms have been considered by a Committee charged with overhauling the selection process. The Committee has recommended that applicants continue to be assessed on the cases they have handled in all superior courts including awards by arbitrators where parties waive confidentiality. They further recommended, however, that applications be vetted by the Legal Practitioners Privileges Committee (LPPC) and that it is the LPPC which should make the final selection. The selection criteria will include evidence demonstrated through decided cases running over a period of 10 years. Any case cited in support of an application must determine issues of serious legal importance and passages in the judgment must disclose how the applicant has contributed to the development of the law in that case. This is intended to deal with the possibility of conflict of interest. A feedback system is also recommended so that each applicant will be kept abreast of the progress of his application at any given time.

The consultation has also been widened so that an applicant will not be recommended until judges, colleagues and clients have all been consulted. A processing fee will now be required, whereas previously applications were dealt with free of charge. Additional changes include an assessment of the applicant's chambers by the committee for suitability. However, the main difference between the old procedure and the new is that every activity in the selection process, including screening, will be performed by the LPPC itself and not delegated to other bodies such as the Supreme Court Justices

Appointment as a High Court Judge

There is more than one way to join the ranks of the senior judiciary.

Some lawyers join the magistracy shortly after admission and work their way up through the various grades of magistrate until elevation to the higher bench as a High Court judge. Others after a good stint in private practice apply for appointment as a High Court Judge on the basis of their experience and reputation.

There is no "best" way to do this. There are advantages in both approaches. The magistracy route provides substantial and gradual experience in dealing with all sorts of cases in all types of court. On the other hand the experience acquired by the advocate in private practice may have been attained in High Courts and above which could provide detailed prior understanding of the process of proceeding in such courts and also of the tricks of advocates at the higher level. On the other hand he or she will have less experience of the necessary judging skills, such as managing a court.

The requirements vary from one state to the next but in all cases applicants must have been admitted for a minimum of ten years and must be of good standing with the Supreme Court and the Nigerian Bar Association.

J.B. Daudu SAN kindly responded to questions on changes in the criteria for appointment as an SAN.

Preparing for a job interview and useful tips for women in the workplace

First impressions count – and often make all the difference

Anecdotal evidence from partners and heads of chambers indicates that first impressions do count, indeed far more than most interviewees would imagine and they often make all the difference. In the first minute of the interview an experienced recruiter will have made a lightning assessment of a candidate and formed an opinion on the basis of that assessment. This evaluation may have been unconscious, but when the interviewer is asked to break down the criteria for this instinctive assessment what will usually be listed are handshake, appearance and grooming, articulation, confidence and presence.

How you shake hands speaks volumes about you and if your hanshake is too feminine and limp wristed can be seen as an "invitation to treat" by predatory males. The first and most important point to bear in mind is that you are being interviewed for a position as a lawyer. Your gender should be of no consequence in this situation, but it could be seen as a weakness rather than a strength if your potential boss can see you only or mainly as a woman in need of protection. Except where it is unacceptable for religious reasons, offer your hand confidently when you are introducing yourself or are being introduced to the recruiter. Shake the recruiter's hand firmly, but then release it as soon as the handshake is completed without lingering.

In most work situations your personal appearance and grooming should be of great importance, but this is especially so in a profession that prides itself on its dress code almost as much as its code of conduct. A clean crisp white shirt and a black or dark navy suit is your safest bet. It is not advisable to wear an outfit that exposes large expanses of flesh; this is inappropriate for the work place in most countries and certainly in a conservative country like Nigeria it is even more so. Polish your shoes and carry a neat handbag. Do not put papers in plastic shopping bags. Do not chew gum or use too much perfume, and be discreet in the amount and type of jewellery and makeup that you employ. Trim your nails and paint them a neutral colour. Pay attention to your hair and ensure that it is styled neatly whether in braids, natural or permed. An interview is not the occasion for multi coloured kinky braids. And finally to ensure that you do not arrive all creased and sweaty for your interview, try to travel in comfort.

Words and confidence

Words are the equivalent to lawyers of a hammer to a carpenter. They are his tools. An inarticulate lawyer is like a carpenter without a hammer. You must make every effort to improve your command of English, which is after all our de facto lingua franca, and your general articulation and fluency. You can increase your vocabulary very quickly and effectively by keeping a dictionary to hand and making a point of learning 10 new words every day. Being able to recite dictionary meanings is not enough; try out your new words in various different sentences, and find at least three different ways of using each one. Playing a word game such as Scrabble with your friends is another simple and sociable way to improve your vocabulary and your understanding of how English works.

Most women are taught to be self effacing and shyness is generally seen as a virtue in most Nigerian cultures. This may be all very well for a woman in private life, but it is not an asset in a lawyer. If you are naturally shy and retiring you need to learn to put aside your private persona and to put on a cloak of confidence. You may not feel confident, but through practice you can certainly learn to give the appearance of confidence, and that is what matters. No one can see what you are really feeling inside. You will look confident if you look people straight in the eye when speaking or listening to them. Be aware of your body and try to sit in a relaxed and comfortable way; keeping your hands folded on your lap will help you to avoid fidgeting. It will also give you the appearance of someone who is in control and who knows what she is about.

The other area that tends to let us down is the speaking voice which invariably betrays our nervousness if not properly modulated and controlled. There are simple breathing exercises which assist with controlling the give away squeak of nervousness and it is advisable to practise these many times before the interview.

The suggestions outlined above are not all that there is to say on the subject of self-presentation and confidence. There are many sources of more detailed information to assist you with making the best impression at interview and at work. Many self-help books have been written on the topic, but the best source of information is often an older woman, whether or not a lawyer, who is already involved in the world of work. Don't be afraid – ask!

The substantive interview

If you breeze through the lightning assessment, but you have no substance, you will still fail at interview, so it is of vital importance that you do not make false claims in the curriculum vitae that you have sent to the interviewer beforehand. You will be asked questions about what you have claimed in your CV. Some of the questions will to some extent be merely conversational, designed to find out a little more about your ability to communicate and get on with people, but others will be directed at establishing whether the claims that you have made are true. Even if your interviewer is not a specialist in the area of Law under discussion, he or she will usually be knowledgeable enough to catch you out.

When you are asked a question, answer as fully as possible, giving specific examples and explanations. The interviewer's nightmare is the monosyllabic candidate who has to be prompted to speak. Think of your CV as the headlines in a newspaper, and see the interview as your opportunity to tell the full story. Most interviewers will lose patience if they are continuously having to prompt the candidate and your interview may come to an abrupt end for this reason alone. If you do not understand the question, ask for clarification rather than waffling.

Again be very conscious of your body language. Don't simper or giggle. Look the interviewer straight in the eye and speak in a confident voice. It is important to remember that there is a very thin line between respect and deference. You are supposed to be a professional, albeit a young one, and should be respectful without being overly deferential. An interviewer will look out for this trait in a candidate. Can you stand up to the stereotypical "pot bellied old chief" who reacts like a raging bull when given unpalatable facts by his lawyer?

Preparation

Preparation is essential for success. You will not win cases for your client if you are not prepared, and you will not even get the opportunity to prepare for your clients if you do not prepare yourself for your interview in the first place.

You must take the time to find out about the chambers or firm who are interviewing you, and acquaint yourself with the work and profile of the senior partners in the organisation. If you know in advance the name of the people who are likely to be interviewing you, take time to find out as much about them as you possibly can.

You should also undertake a trial run to the place of the interview so that you can make a proper estimate of the time it will take to get there. The time of your interviewers is valuable, and it will prejudice them against you even before you meet, if you have kept them waiting for you. They will have spent time preparing for you, and expect you to do them the courtesy of being punctual, and if possible early and unflustered. If your interview is in Lagos or Port Harcourt allocate at least an hour more than you anticipate to allow for adverse traffic conditions.

Honourable Justice
Fati Lami Abubakar
page 40

Funke Adekoya SAN
page 56

Sena Donata
Anthony
page 76

...u Aisha
...assan Baba
...ge 84

Honourable Justice
Rahila Hadea Cudjoe
page 96

Ameze Guobadia
page 104

Priscilla Olabori
Aderonke Kuye
page 116

...yo Obe
...ge 128

Honourable Justice
Mary Ukaego
Peter-Odili
page 140

Justina Anayo
Offiah SAN
page 150

Geraldine
Ekanem Oku
page 164

Oluyinka Osayame
Omorogbe
page 176

Amina Oyagbola
page 190

Sally Olayinka
Udoma
page 206

publishing